Haber Nant Llan Nerch Freit

Haber Nant Llan Nerch Freit
An upbringing on a Radnorshire hill farm

by
George F. Lewis

Logaston Press

LOGASTON PRESS
Little Logaston Woonton Almeley
Herefordshire HR3 6QH

First published by Logaston Press 1998
Reprinted 1999
Copyright © George F. Lewis 1998

ISBN 1 873827 25 3

Set in Baskerville by Logaston Press
and printed in Great Britain by
Hillman Printers, Frome

Contents

Acknowledgements

I would like to thank many people for their help in encouraging and seeing this book take shape. In particular I would like to thank from Llanbister, for a combination of information and in tracking down and finding photographs, Mr. and Mrs. Bennett of Bron-yr-Efail, Mr. and Mrs. J. Bennett of Llannerchfraith, Mrs. O. Bowen, Percy Bowen, Gibson Hughes, Mrs. C. Lewis, Mrs. N. Morgan, Mrs. M. Price, Mrs. Phoebe Reynolds, Mr. and Mrs. B. Thomas, and Mrs. Janet Thomas; and from Crossgates and Penybont Miss P. Bufton, Mr. and Mrs. F. Lawrence, Mrs. Haydn Lewis, Mrs. S. Lewis, and Mr. and Mrs. M. Williams; also Mr. J. Baird-Murray of The Metropole Hotel, Llandrindod Wells and Mrs. Baird-Murray; Mr. and Mrs. E. Beaumont; M. and V. Kendric; my cousin Mrs. C. Lewis; Castle Hill Books of Llandrindod Wells; Newbridge on Wye Antiques; and Brian Byron of Archaeological Investigations Ltd. of Hereford for drawing the maps of the farm and Llanbister village. I would also like to thank the staff of Powys County Library Service, of the County Archives, and of Acton Scott Working Farm Museum.

I would also like to thank various members of my family, including Shirley, Ann and Den, Donna and Karen. Last but certainly not least, I would like to thank my wife, Vera, who has had to put up with a lot of inconvenience and has supported me all the way, and I would like to dedicate this book to her in appreciation.

*My parents on their wedding day, Christmas 1918, with (inset top left)
my mother in later life, and (inset top right) my sister Gwen*

Foreword

All the material in this book is from memory—of family life, school, the farm and the hill behind it, a hill which seemed to symbolize everything solid and everlasting. It was to cast its shadow over my life, both physically and mentally.

I have avoided any fabrication, likewise exaggeration or romanticising. Some memories my be hard to believe when contrasted with the conditions obtaining at the present time, but I assure you that they are accurate.

Even though they tell of a primitive life, we, as a family, were considerably better off than many of our contemporaries. Also my parents believed in the best education that could be afforded, though unfortunately 'Secondary' schooling was out of the question. To make up for it as best they could, a constant stream of secondhand books of every description were bought for us, sometimes a large bundle for a shilling. I was also fortunate that the hired hand took a delight in teaching me before I went to school so that I had more than a head start.

The area was very isolated and until the railway reached Penybont (and that was a day's return journey from the farm by horse and cart) it was at least twenty years behind the rest of the country. Even then it still lagged behind and though these pages tell of the 1920s, the methods and conditions were those of several years before.

This is not to say that the people were unhappy. Quite the opposite. With few exceptions they were self-sufficient and content to leave it at that. It was literally a case of what you never have you never miss.

Rapid progress in later years has sadly destroyed the old community spirit in the country district and village. Not that I would advocate a return to the conditions of those days, but I feel a lot has been lost that is irretrievable. This book is at least an attempt to recall those years and that community spirit, a story of a period in the life of a hill farm, remote and untroubled.

Even now traffic noise is distant if even heard, except for the sound of farm tractors going about their daily work. At the time which concerns us no vehicle had reached the farm except a motorcycle and that in itself was no mean feat.

The farm is Llannerchfraith, which I think is the correct spelling as I will attempt to prove. First mentioned in a charter to the Cistercian monks of Abbey-cwm-hir in the 12th century, it comprised one of the outlying farms of their estate under the name Haber Nant Llan Nerch Freit. The Haber, or Aber, is the mouth or emptying of a stream, Nant is stream, Llan Nerch is a glade, and Freit is mottled. A rough translation would therefore read 'the mottled glade at the mouth of a stream'.

From the monks the ownership of the Abbey-cwm-hir estate passed to the Fowlers. But Llannerchfraith must have become separated from the estate at some point, for when a Mr. Wilson bought the estate from the Fowler family in 1821, he subsequently purchased Llannerchfraith from a Holmes and Worledge in 1824. Mr. Wilson set about improving the property and had a lot of roads made so as to benefit the neighbourhood as well as his own estate, paying the whole cost where the road was in his estate and half the cost from the edge of the estate to where the road joins the Newtown to Llandrindod Wells road at a place always termed the Abbey Turn. A lot of rebuilding took place including what became the farmhouse and buildings, and a stone in the south-west corner of the house bears the inscription RB 1837.

Sadly, financial disaster forced Mr. Wilson to sell in that year, when it was bought by Francis Phillips and his heir was the owner of the farm for the first few years of my family's tenancy. Nothing but good could be said of him as a landlord.

My father purchased the farm in the 1920s and sold it in 1930 to the Bennett family who have been there ever since.

George F. Lewis,
April 1998

SUNRISE

I stood upon a hilltop high
Half way from earth to sky,
And gaze upon the dim dark world
And think 'How small am I?'

Just like a welcome letter
Or see a flag unfurled,
To be on a hill at sunrise
At the awakening of a world.

The darkness swift receding
As the sun at last appears
Dewdrops all a-sparkle
Just like angels tears.

The wind a-blowing through my hair,
The sun upon my cheek
I see a Buzzard floating by,
And think 'I am so weak.'

Be that always as it may,
The world is at my feet,
Beneath the earth, the sky above
And ne'er the twain shall meet.

And then upon the hill I think
Though weak and small may be,
Three is company for all time,
The Earth,The Sky and me.

George F. Lewis

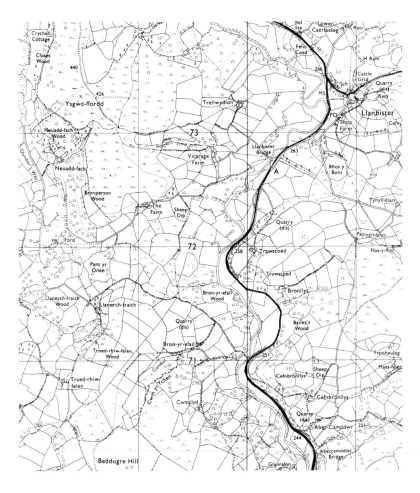

Llanbister and the Ithon Valley,
showing the farm of Llannerchfraith to the south-west of the village

(Reproduced from Pathfinder 949 Ordnance Survey map with the permission of The Controller of Her
Majesty's Stationery Office, © Crown Copyright License No MC88159M0001)

CHAPTER I
The Farm

It's rumoured that a tunnel runs from the Cistercian abbey at Abbey-cwm-hir to the farm, for the monks to use if they needed to escape. On the farm we once found a piece of slate having the carving 'MARH 1659' and wondered whether this had been done by the monks, but it couldn't have been, for the abbey ended its life with the Dissolution in 1538.

The farm was built of stone, walls thick and strong, keeping the cold out in winter yet remaining cool in summer. Its position was similar to that of many hill farms. The buildings were on the flat close to the slope, with the house a little up the steep on what was virtually a step cut in the hillside and, as was the case here, the garden on the next step above. This made for dark back rooms on the ground floor, with the garden only visible from the back bedrooms. Looking at the front it just had five windows—three up, two down—with a porch central to them and a slate roof with chimneys at each end.

The house was not entered by the front door. This was never opened to my knowledge to admit a caller or visitor, conversely I don't remember any caller who expected it or merited it for that matter. Everyday folks knew where the back door was and went directly to it.

This back door, until the drains were laid and concrete put on top, was reached over living rock, worn into holes where the water stood in wet weather, a real collecting place for the soil that was washed down from the steep bank of the cutting that rose to the height of the bedroom windows and to the level of the garden. A heap of bracken lay near the door on which to wipe your boots and, if you were lucky, a yard broom to administer the final touch.

The heavy latched door opened inwards into the 'back kitchen', dark because of the bank at the rear of the house. On the right was the sink cut out of a solid block of stone, ideal for sharpening kitchen and carving knives. Its drain led under the house and emptied itself down the bank and onto the farmyard. Above the sink was an iron-framed window with the ironwork of the two top panes bending through each other to form an arched pattern. This was an indication that this was one of the houses on the estate to which the farm belonged. The window had a deep cill, adding to the darkness of the room, but it had its purpose—the room was lovely and cool on the hottest of days in the summer time. By the sink there was a Dundee china marmalade jar with a shaving brush up-ended in it and alongside a glass jam jar of tooth brushes and a flat tin of Gibbs solidified toothpaste, together with a mirror and assorted soap dishes and packets of washing powder. This was also the convenient dumping place for any small article that would be wanted shortly, later on, tonight, tomorrow or next week.

Past the sink was a door which opened into the dairy. This was the cold store for the milk and cream, the place for the churn and churning, and for a little cheese making when a surplus of milk occurred in spring and summer. The room had a similar small window in the back wall and likewise remained cool in summer. Here lay the locally quarried salting stone, a stone slab large enough to take the sides and hams of the bacon pig for salting to provide bacon for the year. The stone was set into the wall and was supported on two low walls and sloped to one corner to aid drainage. The room was lined with shelves on which jams, bottled fruit and pickles were stored. In one corner sat two logs with hollows cut in them to take the barrel of harvest cider. This was about the only luxury that was permitted, but it had its own logic— a farmer who had a barrel of cider was likely to get a better hired lad than a farmer who did not. At least it was a good excuse and they stuck to it!

But it was the kitchen that was the nerve centre of the house. It doubled up as dining room, sitting room, and school room and was full of functional furniture made from oak by local craftsmen. The main feature was the inglenook fireplace, its black-tarred surround topped off with a mantelshelf running most of the distance of the chimney wall. This fireplace was the most important place in the

The farmhouse, with its ile, the lean-to, on the end

house. It cooked, it heated, it warmed, it was used for reviving lambs suffering from exposure, for making gruel for sick animals and for poultices if they were needed. The recess was some 8 to 9 feet wide, 6 feet high and about 5 feet deep, stone-built and surrounded on the outside by wood with mouldings that were more or less filled from being painted over and over again in the course of many years. On the left of the inglenook was a walled up section that ran from floor to attic, a possible hiding place, that remained after the house was rebuilt in the 1830s.

The mantelshelf above the fireplace was the resting place of a variety of containers which grew into place rather than being put there. Centre of all was the tea tin, not caddy, with a harvest scene which was cleverly designed so that it ran around and around the tin with no beginning and no end. At least it had been so, but through use some of the paint had worn off, but still the wagon load of grain kept going on and on. There were also two biscuit tins. One contained an endless supply of buttons, hair grips, needles, buckles, bandages, and Zam-buc (a universal cure for cuts, bruises, chilblains, sore heels, or even heads for that matter—a placebo that, if it didn't do any good at least wouldn't do any harm, and in many instances was used to help restore peace and quiet). I remember the tin also containing pot menders, old coins, bifurcated rivets, pen nibs and all manner of bits and pieces that could not find a home anywhere else.

Immediately on the left, the grandfather clock ticked away the hours, not loudly but in such a way as to be soothing and restful— almost the same way that fish swimming in an aquarium have. It was made from oak cut less than a mile away and has not moved more than five or six miles in over a hundred years. It was wound every night as the last job before going to bed. The face was white enamel with Roman numerals and little pictures in the corners. Above was what could be called a false front decorated with three cast figures of eagles, but only two brass knobs. Apparently one day when the then three brasses were being cleaned, I fancied a ball to play with and, as is the way of things, left it where it was when the fun was over, which happened to be outside. Unfortunately the first living thing to come that way was the bacon pig and pigs being pigs she took a fancy to my 'ball'. The knob as far as I know is still in existence, but when a pig has failed to eat something the object loses its shape somewhat, and that is particularly true of a hollow brass ball. The clock was required to be a good timekeeper for we had no way of checking the time except when someone came by with a watch, notably the postman who was a source of much news and information.

The grandfather clock, with its one missing brass 'ball'

4

The American clock, and china dogs from the dresser

On the right was the oak dresser, furnished with willow-pattern plates with a few hunting scenes for variety. Large carving dishes were placed on the top shelf, with dinner plates below and tea plates on the lowest. On the very top, above the plates, was a variety of china objects including a pair of small dogs and some decorative fruit. At either end was an earthenware cup of about half pint capacity and shaped like a short-stemmed wine glass, with a cream base colour and an inch wide rich brown band around the top, crazed with age, each in fact a cider cup.

On the lower part of the dresser sat another two biscuit tins, these doing duty as a filing system. One contained letters and forms still to be dealt with, whilst the other held the ones that had been answered. It must be said that the need for forms and correspondence was minimal as compared to the present day, so that these tins were sufficient for a whole year's private and business correspondence. This lower section also housed three drawers: Mother's drawer, the Girls' drawer and the Boys' drawer; father had to share with mother. The whole stood on four slender legs that always seemed inadequate to me.

Under the window was the bench which sat four. In front of it stood the table with three standard kitchen chairs, but next to the top end, though still to the side, was 'Dad's' chair, bigger than the others as befits the Master's chair. This was a carver, with large curved arms and turned legs, chosen for comfort, and moved from the table to the fireside as required.

There is an apocryphal story about just such a chair. One day a young man, probably the neighbouring farmer's son, called on a matter of business (though there is some doubt about this as the farmer in question had quite a smart daughter), and sat in this most important chair to await the farmer's return. When he arrived, the young man jumped up and asked 'Am I in your chair, Mr. Jones.'

Mr. Jones replied 'The chairs are all mine, boy', so implying that he was a man of means and if the young man had come courting his daughter then he had to show that he was likely to become the same.

At the top end, nearest to the fire, which also meant the tea pot and the oven and all the duties that went with it, was 'Mum's' chair, a multi-purpose chair if ever there was one. Feed the baby, rock it to sleep, dining chair, serve the meals, forty winks on a Sunday afternoon, turn it about and a fireside chair. Overhead was the 'cratch', a wooden frame on which the year's supply of home cured bacon was stored until required.

On the back wall, furthest from the fire, was the harmonium. With the wireless being something only heard of and still a wonderful mystery, the harmonium was the means of making music and it served to create many hours of enjoyment, and also helped us appreciate music. Mother played whilst Dad sang. Dad had at one time taught singing with a tuning fork, using the Tonic Solfa method, as opposed to Staff Notation, which singers of the time found easier to read. It meant we all had a good grounding in music.

Off the kitchen lay the tiny pantry. After a lot of rain or a very heavy thunderstorm, water would pour out through the rock into the pantry, and under the door into the kitchen. If there was a danger of this happening at night, we left our shoes on the bottom step of the staircase. When a better drainage system was installed this problem was cured, but it still surprises me that such a nuisance was endured for near enough two centuries.

Downstairs was also the parlour, but by name only. With a stone floor, rather damp walls and only a small bedroom type firegrate, far too small to warm the room, it was instead used to store feed-stuffs against the inner walls with the floor kept clear for our use as a play room if it was too wet or cold for us to go outside.

Upstairs, leading off the landing, were five bedrooms: the Boys, the Girls, the hired man's, the 'best room' (reserved for visitors) and Mum and Dad's (where I was born), the latter two having a grand view over the farm buildings and land.

My first bed was made of solid oak, with posts four inches square, all surmounted by turned wooden knobs which, by dint of much wriggling and patience, my brother and I could ease out of their sockets and use them as playthings.

The sides of the bed were of oak, polished from use, nailed to which were strips of canvas to support the home-made mattress. Oat straw was twisted into a soft rope-like form which was then woven and cut to the size of the bed. It was then covered with cloth and 'buttoned' using a packing needle and a piece of string. A button was tied on the end of the string, then the needle was pushed through the depth of the mattress and out the far side where another button was threaded on the end. The string was pulled tight through the button and knotted. This was repeated at about nine inch intervals until the whole mattress had been done and which prevented the contents from moving about and becoming uneven. Not a very comfortable bed you might think, and you would be right, so a feather bed was the answer.

When the geese were dressed at Christmas the feathers were all carefully collected and kept for this purpose, and once enough were available, a feather bed was made. Feathers have a nasty habit of finding their way through anything but the hardest and closest cloth so 'Ticking' had to be bought. It was stitched up to the size of the bed, and while still inside-out was rubbed with common household soap, or better still bees' wax, to 'fill' the weave so as to form an extra barrier to prevent the escape of the feathers. The ticking was then turned right side out and stitched until only a small hole was left to fill it with feathers. Once filled, a further cover, perhaps of un-bleached linen or, if money wasn't too tight, something better, was put over it to make the final mattress.

There was no bathroom, but we had the fountain—two and a half gallons of boiling water was enough to have a good bath, though it wasn't that convenient and it meant we took fewer baths than perhaps we should. The younger fry got away lightly in the summer time by taking a lump of soap (you mind you bring it back with you!) to the river, and letting the water come to us.

The fountain was a cast iron container about 10 inches in diameter and maybe 18 inches tall, sides upright so far with sloping

A pan, the fountain and dinner pot standing on the pig bench,
with the milk tin in front

shoulders and a dome-shaped lid topped with a brass knob. Hot water was drawn off by means of a tap which extended about 6 inches from the base. The tap was polished to perfection, as was the knob on the lid.

It was an unwritten law that anyone taking some hot water for the bath tub was duty bound to replace it with cold (the equivalent law also applied to the water bucket, milk jug, sugar basin, coal bucket and firewood container); the only exception being when there was a danger of the fountain being over-filled. The fountain then had to be lowered on the sway onto the fire to bring it back up to heat. But the job didn't always end there. If the fire had burned low it followed that it had to be made up—just your luck! As soon as it boiled it did a 'James Watt', or so we called it. The steam raised the lid and when the pressure was released it fell back creating quite a clatter, telling you that it was boiling and which necessitated turning the lid slightly and putting the fountain up a notch or so on the sway. Crude it may seem in our modern world, but it meant there was always water on tap, except for first thing in the morning, but then washing in cold water first thing was better than any other method of getting you fully awake.

The lean-to on the south end of the farmhouse was called the Ile and was originally the stable for the pony, but later became the coal store (one ton per year!) and the home for all sorts of tools, oddments and the sheepdogs.

All the level area in front of the house was covered in green grass, and even in winter the ground was firm and dry and as such was a ready-made and always available playground. When drains were laid at the back of the house, the opportunity was taken to build a retaining wall and lay concrete. This gave us a somewhat narrow football or cricket area that was always usable except when the whole area filled with snow.

The nearest farm building to the house was a sort of two up two down arrangement without a stairway. The lower floor had two entrances at the front which were at the level of the farmyard, whilst the upper rooms had their entrance on the opposite side of the building from the top of the slope. The lower storey housed the pigs and ducks, the upper the hens and a soil toilet—rather primitive but cost effective, the prime requirement in those days.

The farm buildings proper were built between 1833 and 1850 by the then landlord, Francis Phillips. They were more or less on the square with the house and contained the usual mix of cow houses, calf pen, stable and barn, sadly inadequate for the number

Farmyard and buildings in Winter, looking south

9

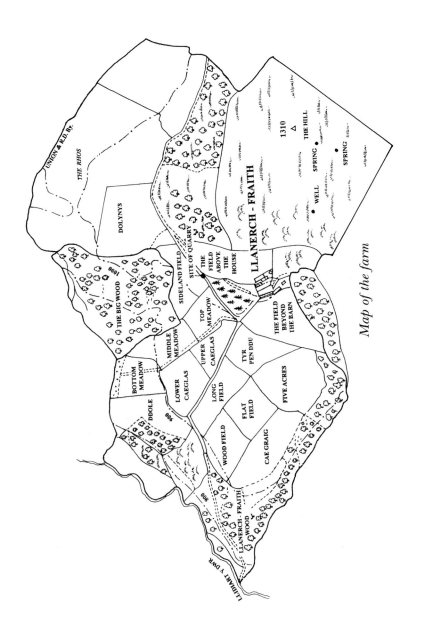

Map of the farm

of animals that were kept—a direct result of the shortage of cash that a was a never ending worry. Food and clothing had to have priority.

Above the high level garden lay 'The Field above the House'— quite steep, but not too steep for cultivation. Up to the top and climb through the wire fence, and it was out on to the open hill, bracken and gorse, with an occasional outcrop of rock or stone. The hill was very steep from here on, so it was best to climb it at an angle; anyone who started straight up generally changed their mind and direction before long. The top is very level, with mounds and hollows that tell tales of long gone. One such mound, maybe twenty yards across, proved on investigation to consist of stone overgrown with grass of the type that grew on the hill. Not far from this spot there was a hollow where water welled up and, being on the edge of the steep, people had excavated the area and made an earth dam. Why, I don't know as just a small pond would have been sufficient for normal use. There was a road of sorts on the north side of the hill that the hill dwellers used, also what appeared to be a packhorse path on the west. As the packhorse way leads to the old mound of stone, perhaps this marks the remains of an old windmill to which the horses were carrying grain. But who these people were and why they lived up here I don't really know, but there certainly was a reason or they would not have done it.

It's a lovely spot. The wind, which is very much stronger than down at the house, rushes through the hill grass. This grass is much shorter and very closely packed, the result of many years of grazing by sheep. As you walk across it small birds rise in front and if luck should smile it could be a larger grouse. But you would probably be more frightened than the grouse with the suddenness of it, together with his call of 'Go-back, Go-back, Go-back' as he disappears as quickly as the terrain will allow.

The sheep move away a short distance and eye you suspiciously, realising that you are a stranger and wondering in their animal way what is the best way to deal with the situation. As the dog has been left at home, they soon settle down, some going on grazing, others maybe a little more trusting lie down to chew the cud, but all facing you to keep you under constant observation, their lambs lying with them and facing the same way.

Looking around, you appreciate that whilst it was hard work to get up, it was certainly worth it. The skyline of New York or the lights of Piccadilly don't hold a candle to this. Here is freedom,

Looking over the farm from 'The Field above the House'

freedom to breathe, look, think, enjoy; a place to forget the pressures of life and relax, to lie on the grass and watch the clouds float silently by, looking almost near enough to touch, so clean and white against a sky so blue as to be unreal, deep blue overhead and fading away to the horizon to a paler shade, not so much opposite to the sun as in the southern and western horizons.

Looking south, all hills, trees, animals and even the clouds throw a shadow towards us, so that the bright sun above and the shadows on the ground give quite a contrast, a challenge to any artist as they alter by the moment into different shapes and sizes, almost ethereal in as much that the change is so stealthy like the hands of a clock, seemingly un-moving and then so different a few minutes later. A constantly changing scene, no two moments, no two days and no two years the same. Looking north there are no shadows, whilst both east and west melt into the other as we turn about.

Sometimes, when showers are frequent and heavy and the sunlight strong, shadows and sunlight chase each other across the fields, over the trees, up and down the hills in an endless procession of irregular shapes and one gains an impression of endless motion and a feeling that man, with all his knowledge and power, has no influence over such natural things.

An occasional grey or white spot marks a farmhouse and buildings of our neighbours, friends, or family, so far away but always willing and ready to give a hand if you need one.

Perhaps whilst lying on the hill, a buzzard or even a pair decide to circle and survey the valley using the thermals to fly over a wide area. But the unusual thing is that you are looking down at them. You hardly dare to blink for fear of scaring them off. Eventually they climb up the hillside when you can see that the only movement is of the head and ever so slight adjustment of the tail feathers, a sight never to be forgotten.

The same can be said of the lark. You hear it below you and then it rises and sings its way up past you into the blue to hover and sing. When he deems he's sung his quota, he drops like a stone to disappear into the tall grass at the foot of the slope where probably his mate and youngsters are hiding.

Sometimes, when the wind is strong, the crows can be seen playing in it or, maybe it would be more correct to say, on it. In general, adult animals and birds take life fairly seriously and only indulge in play if conditions are conducive, as with an animal that has been let loose after being confined for any length of time and shows its appreciation, but often this play is short lived and the animals concerned return to their ordinary placid behaviour. Crows act a little differently and will play for quite some time on a strong wind. They approach the hill from the leeward at a fair rate and at the appropriate moment rise into the fast flowing air and are

Looking west from the hill, towards Tyncoed

13

carried skywards in what appears to be an absolutely uncontrolled manner before regaining control to fly back to their starting point. They then carry out the same manoeuvre time and time again, at the same time cawing and calling to each other in much the same way as children.

Another bird which plays is the jacksnipe, but unlike the crow it does so on a clear still night or rather 'the edge of night', a Radnorshire way of saying 'dusk'. The bird flies up to a very considerable height and then descends with wings set so that they vibrate, creating a noise which is audible over a wide area. It then climbs again and repeats the process a number of times. I suppose it is possible that this is not really play, but a way to lay claim to the surrounding territory.

Whether we like it or not, time always has the last word. The sun sets and an occasional light glints in the valley and our thoughts turn to a nice cup of hot tea beside a wide open fire in the grate, the smell of burning logs and the prospect of a long sleep in. As we go down we can mark out the course of some of the nearby tracks and roads. Three lanes served the farm, each could be travelled by horse and cart and each led to a different village. To us the most important was the way to school in Llanbister, three and a half miles away. Unfortunately for us only the last half mile was a county road, the rest being fields and farm roads, 'cart roads' that had never seen a motor vehicle and were for the most part impassable to them anyway.

Another lane led in a more or less southerly direction, passing through the neighbouring farm which bears the name meaning 'At the foot of the brown [or yellow] slope'. This lane passes a second farm and then a lodge which once marked the southern edge of the estate before reaching a county road of broken stone—tarmac had not then reached this far. This particular route was the way to the railway station at Penybont and from there to Llandrindod Wells, the nearest town, at that time a spa of much fame for the variety and healing qualities of its mineral waters.

The road going west is I believe the oldest as it leads to Abbey-cwm-hir where the monastery lay and was the route taken by the monks in their travels to and from the farm. It was also the first road by which a motor vehicle, a motorcycle, reached the farm. This road was narrow and rutted, passing under trees and with overgrown hedges, slowly converging with the river which here flows very fast. This place is called Llidiart-y-dwr, meaning 'gate of the water'. As you approach a gate across the lane almost all noise is drowned by the sound of the river. This is alright by day, but for someone a little nervous and travelling at night it was a different matter and even the stronger characters didn't linger. The gate had what was called a spring latch, much favoured by people on horse-back, the reason being that by using a hooked stick it could be un-fastened and the gate opened without dismounting, the gate being hung in such a way as to close itself after passing through. Once through, the gate was heard to 'bang' shut as it hit the post in closing. But the eerie part was that there was then a slight pause, followed by the sound of the gate gently closing a second time. The general belief was that there was someone or something watching to see who was coming or going, and here again the monks were connected in some sort of ephemeral way. Suffice to say that people who pretended not to place any credence in the story still found another way home after darkness fell.

A logical explanation is quite possible. When the gate shut the first time, it might have gained sufficient momentum so that when it hit the post it rebounded before the spring latch had sufficient time to engage. So the gate reopened a little way before more gently closing, giving the impression that someone else had opened the gate, passed through and shut it quietly. But the spring latch is quite a modern invention, so what gave rise to the story? Was there a guard at this place at one time? Was this something to do with the abbey? When the monks were here was this a sentry-post to warn them of possible danger? I'll never be sure of the answer, but it leaves me with a deep longing and regret at not being able to answer some of the mysterious occurrences that have so long gone unresolved.

The section of this cart track from Llidiart-y-dwr to the farm was steep and wandering, taking the gentler slants to make it easier for the horses when hauling loads to the farm. Some of this road was of the dug-out type, where the soil had been taken away to such a depth that rock or stony material was reached, providing a sound surface, but so often at such a depth that when walking it was not possible to see into the fields on either side. An annual sight on the side of this section was a wild white foxglove which was very much talked about at the time, as there were then few if any variations or mutations about as opposed to the present day.

Whilst the hill was for climbing, as were trees, water was to get wet with, all the more so if it was in a brook. 'And in this brook there was some fish, E.I., E.I.O...../ And in this brook we wet our feet, E. I., E.I.O!' There were bull-heads, trout, tiddlers—pilks we called them—and young salmon, called samlets. The bullhead (also known as bully head or millers thumb) was easily caught in the hands, cupped and closed together under the water, slowly at first and quickly to enclose the fish and a little water. The fish was then placed in a small pool already prepared in the sand where the water filtered in from the stream, and kept for a count at the end of the session.

There was also a small silvery fish about three inches long and having four whiskers around its mouth which we called a 'grachau'—gra as in granny, the 'ch' as 'kh' and with a hissing sound, and the 'au' as double 'ee'. I have no way of knowing whether this is a local name or not. Like the bullhead this fish rested under stones and to find them you had to lift the stones very carefully and slowly.

A final count as to who had caught the most, the grachau scoring higher than a bullhead, decided the winner and the fish, frightened no doubt, were put back in the brook from our small pools in the hope that they would provide further sport at a later date.

CHAPTER II
Early Memories

To really understand the events and memories that I record, you need to picture my family. We were a family of seven: mother, father, two boys and three girls. I had one older brother, but all the rest were younger, with ten years between the eldest and youngest of us.

One thing I am certain of is that the order in which you are born, the temperament of the older and the younger and your own reaction has a profound and lasting effect on the whole of your life. My older brother was extremely good to me, but being older he was my superior. He was bigger and to all intents and purposes, wiser. Much the same applied, but in the opposite way, as far as my sisters were concerned.

We operated as a complete unit. I don't want to pretend that we never argued or quarrelled, we did and did a good job of it too, but there was never any animosity or ill feeling and our parents had the good sense to recognize this and left us to our own 'devices' or told us to go and 'fight our own battles'. But it must be said that battles won by any means other than that which was honest brought down the 'Wrath of the Father', to use a little biblical language.

Mother was a gentle, quiet sort of person. She was sympathetic, competent and never spoke an ill word to or about anyone, nor would she allow it or listen to anything of that description, an attitude she shared with my father.

But Dad was different in many ways. He had been reared in a hard school, as the saying goes, and had had to look after himself from an early age, becoming a good businessman, very practical but at the same time quite far seeing.

My father in front of the farmhouse

Whereas mother would scold and coax, Dad would give you one chance and after that you were on your own. If it was the first time you transgressed he would ask 'Why did you do it?'. If you could answer truthfully, 'I didn't think it was wrong', the reply came, 'Very well, but you know now, and you know what to expect next time.'

If you transgressed again you had the birch, a slender rod, administered according to the offence. But first he would ask, 'Do you remember me telling you what would happen if you did the same again?' That was part of the punishment, often worse than the actual birch especially as you had no option but to say yes anyway.

Cruel? No. You deserved what you got and you knew what to expect, and I thank my lucky stars that that was his way. I respected him, as did all us boys and girls. My brother was the adventurous one and got called more often than I and if anyone said anything about it he would say, 'I asked for it, so what?'

I don't remember it of course, but I have been told that I was a very good baby. Since then I acquired a mind of my own and, if the truth is told, at quite an early age too. When you happen to be second to a brother who has already reached that state, you have

My brother Jack and myself, with my sisters Mary and Sybil,
in 1928

the choice of being equal or remaining second for all time, a state
that did not appeal to me even at that early age!

One day, when I had started to talk and get around on my own,
mother was picking gooseberries in the garden and with the gate
shut and a good hedge she felt there was nowhere I could get into
mischief. Eventually she heard me talking to myself (I'm told that
I do it to this day!) and thought no more about it for a while, then
realised that it was going on for longer than usual and came to
investigate. I was by the gate and poking a stick into a hole in the
hedgebank, surrounded by wasps and saying contentedly 'Fies,
Moffs, Bumbees, Lots of 'em'. Needless to say I was grabbed and
carried through the gate at top speed but I wasn't even stung!

Unfortunately, at least so I thought, the situation was such that my parents could not afford new clothes for both of us, so I had to have the clothes and shoes which my brother had out-grown, supplemented by clothes made up from second-hand garments bought for a matter of pence at jumble sales or church bazaars. In a way it was lucky that I was small for my age as it meant that my brother could wear his clothes a little longer and also made certain that by the time that I had finished with them they were well and truly worn out.

This state of affairs also applied to shoes. How well I remember breaking-in those shoes—still too big for me but as my own were worn out I had little choice but wear them. Anyone who has had to walk three miles (the distance to school) in badly fitting footwear will no doubt feel sorry for me. Though I resented it, I have a sneaking

Me aged about 9

feeling that I took comfort from the fact that my brother was faring no better in his brand new shoes and if I could grumble freely and so relieve my feelings, his pride did not allow him to do so.

Let no-one think there was any jealousy or enmity between us, quite the opposite in fact, for if either was in any trouble anywhere we stood back to back without fail. That doesn't mean that we never disagreed, we did, mostly with me on the defensive, but these occasions were of very short duration and without acrimony.

I very clearly remember my first new pair of shoes, the name was stamped in the heel in gold lettering—Little Duke, size 2. Was I proud of them!? The first time I wore them was to Sunday School. It was a hot summer day and part of the path we had to take was the old packhorse track across the side of the hill, and if you have ever tried walking on the side of a steep hill in summer you will know how slippery dry grass can be. Imagine me trying to keep upright in my precious new shoes. Suffice to say that I eventually arrived at Sunday School in a suitably chastened state of mind, but still proud of my new shoes.

Some of my early memories are so clear and vivid that it is hard to believe that they happened so long ago and yet be clearer in my mind than things that happened quite recently. One such is the first airplane that I saw. It came over the hill and could not have been much higher than the summit. No-one could persuade me that there was a man in that 'thing'—it was too small for a man to get into—I said. The flying machine, as it was then called, was a bi-plane with struts and wires between the wings and with a single engine.

I also remember my parents discussing what I now believe to be the passage of a comet. It is so clear to me their saying 'It wouldn't be seen again for another eighty years' and this so puzzled me as to how anything could go away for eighty years and then return. Balanced against my complete faith in what my parents said at all times, this put my reasoning out of kilter for years until I had a little more knowledge of such things. This may seem strange to people now, but even grown-ups then didn't fully understand these things and had no 'use' for them anyway.

At this time the farm was part of a country estate and I remember a day when an oak tree was being felled for estate use in the woods above the river at Llidiart-y-dwr. By the side of the stream there was about fifteen yards of flat before the ground rose very steeply to the tree concerned, which was itself just below the cart track. The intention was to drop the tree across the track for ease of subsequent sawing, but someone miscalculated and the tree toppled the opposite way down the steep where sod's law took a hand and the tree ended up with its top on the flat and its trunk in a near vertical position. Imagine the chagrin and embarrassment of the workmen. Advice was given by everyone, but the only solution that seemed acceptable was to cut the branches as high as possible on one side and if any movement occurred to run for dear life, and if none to go back and repeat the cutting. After many 'cut and runs' the tree gave in and laid its trunk on the ground. But the workmen had to accept many a ribbing about oak trees that grew the wrong way up and stood on their heads.

Some of my memories seem to be of times before it is possible to have a memory, and possibly the recall has been aided by hearing the story told by my parents or some older person. One such incident occurred when I was under five years old.

The flat area in front of the house ended in a steep bank that dropped down to farmyard. On this bank grew mallows and worm-wood, the latter a conditioner fed with chopped oat straw to horses. I had been playing with my brother on this bank and for some unknown reason he left me to my own devices—and this is one of the earliest instances of my being disaster prone. Well, either I wandered into the territory claimed by the geese or the geese into mine, resulting in the gander taking what he considered appro-priate action to defend his charges to my definite danger and possible harm. When mother came running to see what all the noise was about, Turk, the sheepdog, had already come to the rescue and got hold of the gander by the neck, dragging it forcibly down the bank away from me whilst receiving a terrible beating from the gander's wings in the process. The strange thing was that the gander was not harmed, a fact that would seem impossible under the circumstances. I do not remember all the story, but I do recall the gander biting my face and being terribly frightened. I can also still see Turk taking the gander down the bank. This was one of the not so pleasant moments, but these were few and far between.

Toys were home-made and often ingenious. For example, an old cork (not taken from a bottle of wine, I hasten to add!) was placed on the table in such a way as to be nearer the youngest and further from the elder, *pro rata* on an arms length basis, you could say, so as to give all as near possible an equal chance. Then the command 'Grab' was given and the one that got the cork gained a point. The cork was repositioned, or if you like a handicap was applied to even out the chances in the light of experience. Then the person in charge would start talking about almost anything and in mid-sentence, or even in the middle of a word, say 'Grab' loudly, softly or even when turning away from the table.

Whatever was to hand was used to make or play a game—a stick, a stone, a feather, anything that the imagination could use to conjure with. When bored an inventive child's mind will excel all the wisdom of the learned.

For the girls a Rag doll was an absolute must, with head, body, legs and arms made separately, it was stuffed with soft, dried grass and sewn together, with eyes and mouth subsequently added. After a while the stuffing loses its firmness and the limbs in particular become soft and floppy. I was once given one to look after by one of my sisters when we were 'Down the Lane' a favourite place to play, and just for the sake of doing something with it flung it up in the air as high as I could. A limb of a scots pine hung out high above and one of the doll's legs wound itself around it. My sister was in tears and demanded that I get it down, but there simply wasn't anything I could do. Armistice was signed when Dad said that when they brought a load of hay that way he would get it and, as the Bible said, 'It came to pass' and total peace was restored.

For boys there was the cloth ball—suitably shaped pieces of cloth stitched together, turned inside out and stuffed just like the dolls. Both were indoor toys unless the grass was really dry, but later a rubber ball arrived from somewhere and that ended the outside problem.

One toy was top of all—the catapult. The difficulty was getting the elastic, it often having to come from an old piece of inner bicycle tube. Once this was available the rest was simple. A forked stick, generally provided by an ash sapling which dies off at the tip and sprouts two new leaders from buds that are opposite each other, and not alternate as is the case with most other trees, provided the handhold and the forks to hold the elastic. This was tied, in equal lengths, to each fork and to a piece of soft leather which held the pebble.

Then there were the time honoured bow and arrows. Whatever size or age you were a bow and arrow could be tailored to fit. But as the bow got bigger and therefore stronger, the string became relatively weaker. The bow was ash, no other tree had the spring, but it was quite difficult to find an ash sapling of the right thickness along the length of the bow, otherwise the bow was only the strength of the thinner end—an example of the 'weakest link'. Arrows were made from hazel, the nicest, straightest stick in the wood, and of a hundred and one purposes. Feathers were tied with thread in a split in the back end, whilst pieces of sheet iron for tips were tied in at the other end with wire more generally used for making rabbit snares. Again a dangerous toy, but used with care and responsibility that was in itself an education.

A sling was another toy. Two pieces of string, about eighteen inches long, were fastened to the ends of a piece of soft leather about two inches long by one inch wide. The string was held in such a way as it was easy to let one string go and still hold the other, and a pebble was placed in the leather. The sling was then swung in a vertical circle until sufficient centrifugal force was generated. At the desired moment one string was released and the pebble shot out. It was not very accurate—David must have had a lot of practice!

Another missile launcher was made from a hazel stick about eighteen inches long and three-quarters thick, split at one end for about four inches down its length. A stone or pebble was inserted in this split and a forward swing was made which ended against a static object, possibly the free hand, and which would cause the pebble to leave the slot and travel some distance.

Eighteen inch long hazel sticks could also be sharpened at one end and used as throwing knives—often at a target positioned on a bank. Longer sticks made spears and for a similar game.

All these were banned from anywhere near the house and buildings, and pointed arrows were not allowed for 'Cowboys and Indians' at any time.

Stone throwing was a riverside game where there were pebbles galore, and thistles growing on the banks as targets. But there was one 'Don't'—'Don't throw any, and that means *any*, out on the field where they could damage machines or blunt scythes or mower blades.'

Hoops, or Bowlers as they were known locally, were made from about six feet of strong fencing wire, turned into a circle and the ends joined with a little loop. A bit wobbly, but who was worrying about that? This was then pushed or tapped along with a short stick held horizontally—erratic it's true but that was part of the art of playing with it.

Later on the rim of a bicycle wheel turned up, just the rim, no tyre, tube, spokes or centre, but boy what a prize! You stood the wheel upright, held your small stick vertically in the groove in the wheel and pushed. It needed a little practice, but then away you went as fast as you could run, and it was extremely manoeuvrable. Trouble was that there was only one between us, so turns were taken to the spout and back, a distance of about 150 yards. As they say 'It's an ill wind that blows no-one any good,' and when the workman had an accident on his bike, he gave us his buckled front wheel. We didn't mind how many accidents he had if it meant the same again.

About this time our headmaster brought 'Gyro-scope', a toy, to show us in school. I thought that if the spinner on the toy could keep standing on its little tower, why not get the bicycle wheel to do the same? So a stake about two feet high was driven into the ground and a hollow carved in the flat top with a pocket knife. The wheel, this one with spokes and spindle, was then placed in the indentation and spun horizontally, almost like stirring a pot and, lo and behold, it worked, though it did use to fall off quite often!

Who thinks that a frisbee is a modern toy? Battered saucepan lids were used before he was ever thought of, and if they had the handle missing, all the better. If it landed on something hard like a stone, the enamel would break off making little spitting sounds. Thrown from the steep side of the hill with the wind in the right direction the skimmer would travel an amazing distance before reaching the ground.

I acquired a pair of stilts after a lot of asking and maybe doing a few jobs—a pair was left standing by the door with not a word said. These again were made from our good friend the hazel, from a couple of sturdy stems with a strong fork. But a word of warning— don't ever try to walk through the farm pond. I got away very wet, very muddy and very sorry for myself, leaving one stilt standing forlornly in the middle of it. That is until I decided that I was as wet as I could get and waded back in and retrieved it.

Then there was the jumping pole, yet again of hazel, six feet long and strong enough to carry our weight. And there were things galore just waiting to be jumped!

Autumn was the time of the conker, the horse chestnut, threaded on a piece of string salvaged from the weekly delivery of groceries. The first to challenge with 'Ibbly, Ibbly, Ack, My first Smack', proceeded to try to batter the opponent's conker. Kills were religiously counted and a conker with a good score was much mourned at its demise. One method calculated to increase a conker's hardness, and so its potential score, was to bake it lightly in the oven. Some people thought that boring the hole for the string with a red hot nail would serve the same purpose, but these two practices were considered to be not quite fair.

Leaf fall provided a game, hectic and short lived. A large ash tree grew a little distance from the house and often after the first frosty night the wind in the morning was sufficient to bring the leaves down at quite a rate. The game was to catch them before they touched the ground. Easy? Not so, the shape of the leaves make it so that the fall is, to say the least, erratic. The trick was look to see if there was one just floating down nice and steady and go for that one—far better than chasing all and sundry and missing most. It gave a lesson in observation and common sense.

Winter was not the best time of the year, but it had its compensations. The toboggan was one. The field above the house was actually the lower slope of the hill and supplied all that was necessary. Father was persuaded to make a toboggan for us, then we waited for snow or hoar frost—incidentally hoar frost was far the faster of the two. Given the right conditions we didn't show up in the house except when dinner or tea was ready and we didn't have to be persuaded to eat them either! We discovered that dragging something on one side caused the toboggan to veer in that direction, so a hinged lever was fitted on each side and by using these brakes, as we called them, we could steer a certain amount.

The hedge at the bottom of the field joined the orchard which was more level, but from the field through a gap in the hedge there was a drop of somewhere in the region of two feet. As you can guess, we used our steering gear to aim for the gap and if you hit it square on, the momentum carried you forward to land six feet down the orchard. But 'happy landings' in the orchard were a rarity and more often than not toboggan, driver and passenger(s) arrived in the orchard in an absolutely haphazard fashion; thankfully no bones were ever broken.

When hard frost covered the pool with ice, our hob-nailed boots were the perfect medium for sliding. If the weather was too bad for outdoor activities, then the Parlour came into its own and out came the marbles. Large glass ones with pretty designs in the centre were called taws and counted for any number (as desired) of the ordinary marbles. We were always short of marbles, so we made our own. There was what was called a blue clay 'heave', a clay of pasty nature that was forced up into a small stream by underground pres-

Overlooking the farm in winter

sures. This clay was formed into 'marbles' and dried naturally before being placed at the back of the fire, so that they baked gently, and were rescued next morning when the fire was relit. Out of twenty put in the fire it was lucky if eight were serviceable, but there was always plenty of clay and a fire every night. Half the fun was making them, anyway.

But the best toys of all were the dogs, Turk and Rover. Spring, Summer, Autumn or Winter, you could call and the toy would come to you.

Turk was a black and tan and always seemed to be there unless he was called to go to work. As soon as work was done, he found his way back and lay down close by, to all intents and purposes going to sleep. But a close look would discover the occasional partial opening of one eye that closed again.

Rover was somewhat different, young and wild and where I went so did Rover. Throw a stick or a stone and Rover brought it back. He loved to have you put a length of stick in his mouth and, hanging on to the other end, off we ran, Rover growling away. The trouble was that Rover could run faster than you and eventually you 'came off'.

Taking into account all the books that were bought from Church and Jumble sales, we were in no way deprived, and all at very little 'cost', the little word with a very big influence.

A somewhat dangerous game we played was 'Head-over-Heels'. Not a very dangerous game, you may say, but add to that a hillside, steep and dotted with outcrops of rock, gorse, heather and ant hills and make the game 'First to the Bottom!', and the risk factor is multiplied ten times at least. We had worked out a system of giving a distance to the younger ones (our sisters) to even up the chances, and if one (or more) got on their feet and ran we pretended not to have seen it, for that guaranteed another game another day. A bump on the head or a grazed elbow were worthwhile penalties to pay for getting to the bottom first. It was maybe for the best that this was forbidden by our parents when we started on the steeper slopes where we may have done ourselves some physical damage.

Sometimes during Spring or Autumn there would be a night with a full moon, when the skies were clear and boys and girls came out to play, as the old adage goes. Two brothers and three sisters were all that was necessary. The light and time, and being allowed to go out to play when we were usually in bed made it special, apart from the fact that it happened only about twice a year, three times at the most.

Imagine that you are standing on a nice patch of ground with the moon shining on the house, reflections in the windows, shadows under the eaves and from the chimneys and porch, and there in front of your eyes is a fairyland house and home where there is everything you want in the world.

It is a balmy night, full moon in a cloudless sky, house and buildings clearly seen but again with that ethereal quality of light and shadow, fields silvered with shadowed hedgerows and trees all helping to instill a certain magic that is so noticeably missing in daylight. Is there any wonder that our play was special?

If it is Spring and the play lapses, take time to look about and take notice, then you may hear an owl hooting and if you are lucky you see one sweep from the trees and into the barn to a nest up on the crossbeams where there are two white fluffy owlets.

Or maybe the mating calls of a pair of foxes, the dog three sharp yapping barks at spaced intervals, answered by the intermittent howl of the vixen, rather an uncomfortable sort of call and answer.

But the badgers, they come into a different category altogether. Their mating call turns a beautiful moonlight night into an eerie scene and sends us into the house out of the sound of them.

Imagine an idyllic night suddenly ended by the most horrible sound that nature has produced, and how such a sound can be used by an animal in courtship beggars understanding. I can only describe it as the sound of a baby or small child in terrible pain and distress past all reason, almost human, yet animal. I still have a chill feel even when writing and trying to describe it.

Some of these happenings seem long ago and others as if they were just yesterday. In the house our play room was the parlour, that rather damp, stone-floored room with thick stone walls, cool in Summer and not too cold in winter when a fire was lit in the small grate. In this play room ended one of my childhood ambitions.

We sometimes went with our parents to Chapel, not that we were very thrilled about it but at least it was better than staying at home. The preacher was a Mr. Owens, who started his sermon gently and with all due reverence, gradually gaining power and acceleration until finally reaching a dramatic climax of what we could expect from any backsliding, unless we followed his instructions implicitly. This was emphasised with his arms thrust upwards and brought down onto the pulpit until the Bible jumped up in the air and the paraffin lamps on both sides flickered and threatened to go out. Then he sat down so abruptly that, being a very small person, he almost disappeared. Needless to say that as children we waited for this event from the moment that he began his sermon.

Well here is the kernel of the nut. In our playroom the firegrate was quite small and low and by using a small household set of steps we could climb up and stand on the mantelshelf. I duly climbed the steps up to my 'pulpit' on the mantelshelf, looked around my congregation of four and proceeded with my 'discourse', to conclude with a suitable 'hands-above-head' gesture, bringing them down to my sides before sitting down. My pulpit being only six inches wide, my bottom hit the wall and I plunged floorwards and lost all interest in the proceedings to the great dismay of my congregation and my mother. Suffice to say that on recovery I seemed to have lost all ambition to be a preacher.

Sunday School always finished with the superintendent offering a prayer, and every time he knelt down to say it, we became transfixed on his nose, as a drop always formed at the end of it. Instead of keeping our eyes closed, as we were supposed to, we stared through eyelashes guessing whether this week the drop would fall off before the prayer was complete.

The charabanc

Another vivid memory is a Sunday School trip. We went to Sunday School most weeks and at the end of each lesson we gave a penny which was used to finance 'The Trip'. This momentous occasion took place in the summer, a charabanc was engaged for the journey to Aberystwyth—well over 40 miles away would you believe! This vehicle did not have a fixed roof, but a collapsible canvas top that folded right back to rest on the back of the charabanc where it was held in place with leather straps. This left everyone to enjoy the lovely fresh air as we progressed towards Aberystwyth at the magnificent and exhilarating speed of 25 miles an hour, except up Plinlimon, and who could expect to climb a mountain at 25 miles an hour anyway! It got a little hot under the bonnet, but nothing that a ten minutes stop would not cure. What a clever man the driver was! Not only could he drive a charabanc, but he knew what to do if it went wrong. On the spot I decided to drive a charabanc or die in the attempt. Mobile again, but Plinlimon like all mountains has the last word, and from nowhere down comes a shower of rain. Panic stations. Pull into the side of the road, up gets the driver, runs down the aisle, grabs the straps and undoes them as quick as he can, too heavy for one, so everyone jumps up, gets in everybody's way including the driver, but patience has its own reward and the top soon gets fixed, everyone a little wet and lo and behold, the sun shines out again—the mountain has the last laugh. We all recover our good spirits and, look out Aberystwyth, here we come.

The old school

Lunch is provided at a good class cafe and we are given a little instruction as to manners when eating out so as not to cause any embarrassment to parents and teachers. Lunch over, it's 'Where's Woolworths?' Nothing over sixpence. A comb for tuppence, a full size comb threppence, a cap gun a tanner (sixpence) and a roll of caps for the gun, one penny. So I decide on a gun and some caps. This gun gave me hours of pleasure, especially after dark when the flash from the caps could be seen. Then the sea, a paddle for most, bathe for those who were lucky enough to have bathing suits and those who hadn't pretending that they didn't want to anyway!

Finally back to the charabanc and head for home, soon asleep. The moon could shine, the rain could fall, we were satisfied, tired and happy, with many days of cowboys and indians to come.

In fact many memories are associated with school. The school was a good three miles from the farm and the way lay across fields and tracks, with only the last half mile on made up road.

So the only way to get there was to walk—rain, hail or sun. My father took my brother and I on the pony on the first day, and met us coming back to make sure we knew the way. (My brother had been going to school from our grandparents' house which was much nearer to the school. After that, we walked.

The school was a rectangular room with an apex roof and three crossbeams, almost like a barn. A curtain was hung from one beam making two sections, one for the Infants and the other the Seniors. Artificial lighting was provided by two paraffin lamps suspended from the beams. I remember them having to be lit during a severe thunder storm, but it was impossible to see to read or write with them. Heating was provided by a Tortoise stove in 'our end' and an open fire in 'theirs'. They were lit, in winter only, by the school caretaker, Miss Mary Price of the Turnpike, half an hour before school started and often when we reached the school the doors of both classrooms had to be kept open to get rid of the smoke. They provided a modicum of heat, though not as much as we would have liked, but we had not learned to grumble in those days; what we had we were glad of and left it at that.

The Tortoise was also used to boil a couple of cast iron kettles to make a cup of hot cocoa to go with our sandwiches at dinner time. (Such high-faluting terms as 'lunch break' were left for the 'Toffs'.) It also warmed our hands and dried our clothes if we got wet. If someone had taken away our Tortoise I think there would have been a riot. We thought the world of the thing!

Mrs. Bennett, our teacher, was a motherly, blousy, homely type of person, not very highly qualified but very able. She talked to us in a friendly way during lessons, and often had a circle of the little ones around the stove if the weather was cold or it was too wet to go out to play.

If the morning was wet or snowy the first lesson was around the Tortoise, wettest or youngest nearest to the warmth, gradually shuffling everybody around until all were dry and warm, then all to their seats and 'let battle commence'. I say that jokingly of course, but discipline was a little more evident than when we were around the stove.

One incident that I recall, a little shamefaced maybe, was an occasion when we had been playing 'up Dwrddu', (Blackwater), a little stream also known as the Dorthy, which ran just outside the playground. We were playing 'Jump-the-bruck', or brook, an old way of playing 'Chicken'. Some pools were deeper and wider than others, but you jumped them to avoid being given the 'cowardly custard' label. Although I was shorter of stature I was quite nimble. Also my brother and I practiced at home to avoid either ending up in the water or refusing to jump. Unfortunately one boy whose courage exceeded his capabilities fell short of the far bank. If the pool had been shallow, as was usually the case, it would have meant wet feet and that was no disaster, but he went in nearly up to his waist. Predicament—he had four miles and some to home, so we were left with having to tell Mrs. Bennett. She had him strip and stand by the stove with nothing else on but his overcoat, and him being a growing lad he had to adopt a crouching posture to preserve his dignity!

I tell this more to illustrate the care and help that she was prepared to give to everyone, not only in her own class but for the whole school—one of the best, and I fear no contradiction.

While we were around the stove at playtimes she would talk to us not like a teacher, but more like one of us. She certainly knew more about the people of the district than anyone else. I remember telling her once about a man bringing us a fish which I described in the way of all fishermen and which was actually a salmon taken out of season. Such was her loyalty to us she insisted that it must have been a nice big trout, not realising that trout were out of season as well!

If the weather was wet we could stay in the classroom and do as we liked—within reason of course. Some liked painting, but not me, I hated painting; some liked modelling with plasticine; I liked reading, and at this time we could read aloud if we didn't make too much noise.

One particular playtime I was reading about 'The Little Gingerbread Boy' in which a nice old lady living alone becomes very lonely and decides to make and bake a little gingerbread boy. So she makes up a mixture for gingerbread biscuits, cuts out the shape of the little gingerbread boy that she wanted, pops it into the oven and waits. When the little boy was baked, he shouts. At this point Mrs. Bennett gave the sign that lesson would start, but being so engrossed in the story I carried on reading aloud the words of the little gingerbread boy saying, 'Let me out' in what was virtually dead silence. Needless to say she saw the humour in it.

As I said, I hated painting, or more correctly, I Loathed it. If they had only known, the greatest punishment that could be administered would have been to give me a brush and paper and tell me to paint a flower. But, give me a set of figures, written or mental and they make sense; composition, how many pages do you want?, and give me a book and time stands still.

My parents set great store in education and started us all off as well as they could, taking into account the little time they had to teach us. Also the waggoner, Ted, used to delight in teaching me the alphabet, times tables and simple sums, so that before I went to school I was ahead of most of my age and I did not go until I was nearly six years old. One day one of the seniors was found to be unable to say the nine times table and I had to go and say it for her! Did it give my ego a boost? You bet!

Strangely enough, this was an early indication of the course of my whole school life, that and the fact that I was so small for my age. One thing I would not do is fight. I couldn't see any sense or reason for it, and anyone matched with someone twice their size or years younger is either hopeless or degrading. Not that I was a physical coward, I suffered many a licking and had to put up with it. As it has been from time immemorial, the big are the physical masters, but the small have to use their brains and claim an ascendancy in the intellectual field. A division between the intellectual and the athletic occurs and forms two distinct types of people which, to put it crudely, meant you were designated either a pugilist or academician according to size or ability. Often this division cut right across families, neighbours, farmers or even professional people and the so-called working class. In effect the social status seems to have had no bearing at all. These divisions often disappeared after leaving school for economic and social reasons, more the pity for the potential scholar who has to forego all his ambitions because of this. This was more or less the case as far as I was concerned— where I had to come second in the schoolyard I came first in school, and I plead guilty of many silent pleasures when my erstwhile masters in the yard 'copped' it inside for bad work while I climbed on my pedestal and gloated.

This is not to say that I was bullied, neither did I take any advantage in class, but it is a bit disheartening when one is always the last to be picked for the football team.

At this stage I used to ask a lot of questions, such as 'Did a ball thrown horizontally actually fall at the same rate as one just dropped?' The answers that I received were 'Why bother your head about such things?' or 'What does it really matter?' or 'Such things are for older heads than yours.' But most of our games and play involved throwing balls, sticks or stones. They were the tools of our childhood and I wanted to know why they did what they did. It is as simple as that, only no-one seemed to bother about it. To me there always seemed to be the question of 'why?'

In my early years I have been told that I didn't just ask 'why?', I asked it three times in a row. You try it, it's deadly! Now of course I realise that their answers were the easy way out and I must admit that my absolute faith in older people and teachers in particular was somewhat dented. And of course the question remained.

Mr. and Mrs. Bennett

My ambitions (note the plural) were varied but did not include farming. Oh yes, I liked animals, in fact I become too fond of them for my own peace of mind at times, and also I liked the freedom and self determination that goes with it. But I wanted to be a policeman with a Red Hunter motor cycle, a preacher, (until I fell off the mantelshelf), a bus driver taking people to Aberystwyth, but most of all a schoolmaster. Of course I became a farmer—so much for my grand plans and ambitions.

The object of my ambition to be a schoolmaster was Mr. Bennett. A typical 'Head' of the time, he was tall, spare, bald and wore pince-nez spectacles which, taken together, gave him a sort of aura, rather severe, or austere, but much respected if not admired for his ability in running the school. Even we pupils respected him in some inexplicable way.

Discipline was strict but not overly so, which I think we unknowingly accepted as right and proper. Talking or moving about in class was strictly forbidden unless permission had been given and that was rare indeed. One look over the pince nez was sufficient for the offender to stop mid-syllable, second time the pointed finger and danger point was near.

From the front the school was a very plain structure. Built of stone and painted over with tar as the custom was in those days, it was somewhat intimidating to any prospective young pupil. Perhaps the idea was to put them in a proper state of mind before they even entered the building. The roof was of dark Welsh slate, which enhanced the dour countenance of the building. The only decoration of any sort was the bell-house on the right-hand end of the roof ridge whilst the ridge itself had a crested design that always reminded me of a dragon's back.

The bell was never rung—Mr. Bennett always used a whistle—except by some of the older boys throwing stones at it while Mr. and Mrs. Bennett were having their dinner. Once an owl made its nest in the bell-house, but an owlet fell out of the nest and died. We were all sad, for it was such a lovely, fluffy, white ball.

Inside the porches were pegs where we hung our coats and puttees, leggings or gaiters if the weather was bad or likely to be before we would get home. The pegs were numbered and some had to share as there were more pupils than pegs, giving rise to the inevitable 'How did my coat get on the floor?' and other such rows. Still we all survived!

Occasionally the outer door would be left unfastened, which led to a dog calling by every day on the off chance that this had happened so that it could help itself to one or more pupils' dinner, according to his fancy. Here Mr. and Mrs. Bennett came to the rescue, for they gave anyone who had suffered, dinner up at their house which made everyone jealous and wish that the dog had had theirs instead. They also fed those who occasionally arrived without sandwiches, normally the children of parents whose sole income (through illness or bereavement) was the parish pay of 5 shillings (25p.) per week.

The porches took up half the width of the front, whilst behind the school, in a separate building shielded from view, were 'The BOYS' and 'The GIRLS'. There was no plumbing, just some primitive drainage. In any case there wasn't a flush toilet in the parish, so why should there be one in the school. And what was the caretaker paid for anyway? If a bucket wanted emptying occasionally why should she grumble.

Drinking water was no real problem. Two water cans were provided, holding about three gallons each, and it was the duty of the 'big' boys to fill them from the well, really a brick holding tank in the field behind the school, and woe betide the boys who tried to skip this job.

The school and the yard were surrounded with a thorn hedge, all in all containing about three-quarters of an acre, the top part nearest to the school building being reasonably flat but falling off steeply to the boundary which was the Turnpike hedge.

The flatter part at the top was just bare earth filled with gravel from the river and trodden flat by many feet over a long time. The lower half was sparsely covered with grass that existed rather than grew, getting better as it neared the steep by the boundary, that part getting less trampling.

One event gave rise to many taunts at school. To the north of the farmhouse stood three acres of mostly spruce and larch with a few beech and scots pine. At the far end of this plantation was a quarry from where rock was taken to repair the farm roads. This rock was formed from compressed layers of mud, the thickness depending upon the rate of deposition. Blocks that were hewn from the rock were sometimes of almost geometric precision, but for one reason or another others were spherical or slightly flattened spheres. In other rock types these sometimes contain other stones or gems or crystals.

As the balls in our quarry were apparently formed without heat their centres were empty or just full of dust which had been shielded from pressure during the process of rock formation. The balls varied considerably in size, from just a tiny lump no bigger than the end of one's thumb, to the size of a small football.

One day father and Fred, the hired lad, were 'rising' rock for future use, and father got one of these balls out of the quarry face. It was no use in its present shape, so the hammer was used to break the ball. But when the ball fell apart there appeared to be a frog in the otherwise empty centre of the ball! Neither my father or Fred had anything to gain from the story, and neither were victims of their imagination as both saw it at the same time. And as for the truth, well it is the story as they told it. They were both prepared to swear on oath that it was true and no amount of derision or questioning would ever shake them from the story. I can assure you that Johnny Barleycorn didn't have a hand in it either!

As far as I know there are only two possible answers. One is that at the instant that the stone ball parted, a frog jumped and landed in the hollow in the centre of the stone without being seen. Co-incidence? The other theory, which seems even more impossible, is that the frog had existed in a state of suspended animation right from the time when the rock was formed and had been protected from being crushed to death by the stone ball.

Sadly the stone was broken up and used, because if it had been preserved some sort of tests could have been carried out and a conclusion reached. But as is usual with any happening of this sort, Black Magic is whispered with sidelong looks and carefully worded insinuations as if the person concerned knew more than he was telling. One theory voiced was that the frog was a devil that had been exorcised and condemned to imprisonment in stone for ever, and that the person who had released it would come to no good as he had released evil into the world—as far as it is known, that did not happen!

Be that as it may, as little as possible was subsequently said about it on account of the teller only meeting with derision and disbelief.

The account that got around was used to belittle us and anyone wishing to cause hurt or distress thought it clever to make snide remarks, and this was particularly evident at school.

At one time I was afflicted, if that is the right word, with warts. Big ones, little ones and middle sized ones, they all had one thing in common—they would not go away. All the cures in creation were tried to no avail, the 'country' cures boggling to the imagination: rub them with a black snail and then impale the snail on the thorn of a whitethorn and never go to see it again, for if you do, the spell put on the warts will be broken and the warts will not be cured. As the snail disintegrates so should the warts.

Another was to wait for a black snail to start moving then grab it by its horns and fling it back over your left shoulder. Here again you must not look at the place where the snail fell, then or at any time thereafter.

My warts were snail proof, of that there was no doubt. So something else had to be tried. Cut a potato in half, rub the warts with one half and put the other half in your pocket. Throw away the half rubbed in the warts and tell no-one where this piece of potato is in case they should go and get it and so break the spell. Neither must you, as with the snail 'cures', go to look at the place where it was thrown. When the half of potato you were carrying disintegrated, so should the warts, along with the other half of the potato.

That is where I think I gave up. However, another involved the blacksmith and I'm pretty certain that had you asked the local blacksmith to officiate you would still have your warts and a flea in your ear to boot! The procedure was that the blacksmith tied a horse hair around the wart or warts (and I had so many that it would have taken half a horse's tail), said the correct words of a spell and that would send them away.

Eventually the warts vanished as mysteriously as they had arrived.

It was our schoolmaster who advised us to use smoked glass through which to observe a total eclipse of the sun in 1927. So we smoked some glass over a candle in preparation for an early morning climb up the hill behind the farm as we had been told that a hilltop was the best place from which to observe the eclipse. It was a great adventure! Up to the top of the hill at about six o'clock in the morning and you will have guessed it was summer time. Up on the hill we were literally on top of our world. We saw the sunrise and lit a fire as an extra treat, and reached a sort of seventh heaven.

Then things started to happen. The sun grew darker as if a shadow was coming across it and it was getting colder by the minute. The wind started to blow and blow cold. It got darker, it got colder and windier, it got eerie. I didn't like it, it had a bad feel, evil, reminiscent of witchcraft. I have never had the same feeling since and I certainly don't wish to either. The net result of this incident is that by day the top of the hill is a pleasure to me, but the same place at night is a place I'd rather not visit, even though I am not in the slightest way superstitious. It was as if at the moment of complete darkness everything would be killed.

Be that as it may, the sun came back just as slowly as it went and with it the wind died down and the air warmed up. But I must admit that the journey down the hill was much less exuberant than the journey up.

One winter's day there had been a heavy snowfall following which the weather had become warm and almost cosy and the snow was thawing fairly fast. On the way home from school there was still plenty of snow and we made a big snowman, and I mean a snow Man. We sat him on a large fence post by the road, gave him eyes and mouth, and to prove his masculinity placed a stick in the appropriate position. As the large amount of snow thawed it caused a drip from the piece of stick, but instead of collapsing in the thaw and falling off the post in a short time as we expected, he just kept sitting there. Maybe the day got colder and the thaw slowed, but the result was that quite a few people saw our snowman. Some said 'Disgraceful', some 'Hilarious' and some a 'Work of Art'.

All my memories of the old school are of a happy nature, but as with everything else things have to change, the 'Old giving place to New', not that we always appreciate the new, quite often the reverse and that was the case here.

But in all truth a bigger school was necessary, the old one was overcrowded and inconvenient and unhygienic and that's putting it mildly! So the new school came into being, much bigger, much brighter and in many ways more inviting than the old, but as far as I was concerned it lacked the character, whilst the atmosphere was not only clinical but soulless as well, and was devoid of the affinity that I had for the old.

A fine brick building with big high windows, porches at each end, not Infants and Seniors as at the old, but Boys to the left and Girls to the right, cookery, woodwork, teachers' rooms and three classrooms. Juniors and seniors were divided by a folding partition

The new school in c.1929

with glass panels, the cause of many rapped knuckles on account of Mr. Bennett seeing through and spotting some transgression when the junior teacher's back was turned. The Infants were still presided over by Mrs. Bennett, the juniors by Miss Lloyd and of course Mr. Bennett in the senior classroom.

Out at the back of the school were the playgrounds, boys and girls separated by high railings, though what purpose that was going to serve I don't quite know. Separate toilet facilities certainly, but to segregate boys and girls during play was likely to do more harm than good. Although I have not seen it, I have been told that the dividing fence has been taken away.

The opening ceremony was impressive. The Director of Education, Captain Mostyn, was there to make a speech, plus a whole bevy of local gentry, County Councillors, District Councillors, Parish Councillors, Uncle Tom Cobley and all. We were marshalled in front of the old school and marched up to the new, and I remember that instead of being glad to go into this glorious new school I was sad to leave the old.

The new school smelled of new wood, varnish and paint. No more standing in front of the old tortoise, no more cosy chats with Mrs. Bennett. Gone forever was the homely smoky smell, the smell of drying clothes and plasticine. When we went on that march to the new school we travelled a road that we'd never return.

It was in this new school that I first heard a wireless, 'wire-less' as no lines or wires were necessary. Radios were a later breed. It was on 11th November 1928, Armistice Day, and Mr. Bennett had brought his wireless into school for us to hear the service broadcast from the cenotaph in London. An aerial was slung from Cartref, the school house, and brought in through a window in the seniors and connected to the receiver on his desk. Wires were taken to the loud speaker—a horn similar to the one on the logo of His Master's Voice. By the side of the receiver was a big flat battery with wires going to it, and also what looked to us like a square glass jar. Mr. Bennett said it was an accumulator and was like a small battery that Pugh's, the shop, could charge up when it ran down. It was all a mystery to us, but he went on to explain to us what each part did, and if I had not been too shy to ask for more I would have done so. It was just too wonderful to believe, and I'm not sure that I did until he turned it on. Most likely I made up my mind then that I'd have a wireless when I grew up!

There was one great advantage for me in the new school in the increased variety of lessons. In the old we were more or less confined to the three Rs, with a little history and geography thrown in and, alas and alack, painting.

If I drew or painted anything it was dead from square one. One day a British Legion poppy was put up for us to paint. It consisted of a small black button with a wire fastened to its centre and on this wire was a piece of red cloth cut in the shape of three petals and fastened to the back of the button. Well, I paint my black button, got it round at last but a little bit bigger than I had intended, but never mind, there's plenty of room on the page. Next, three red petals, not too bad really but one was a bit smaller than the other two, so make it a bit bigger. Now it's too big, so I will have to enlarge the others. Now the button that was too big looks a bit small.... You get the picture, and I certainly did, a full page of it!

However, in the new school I could do cane, raffia and leather work instead. But my stay was short, for my family moved to another farm which meant a new school where I stayed until I left at fourteen. Due to economic pressures I had to forego the many ambitions of my childhood and settle down to be a farmer with the best grace that I could muster.

The school still occupies the same site, but where the old school was the Vicarage now stands. But whatever happens the Old School will always be there in my memory.

CHAPTER III
Farming

Although the years referred to in this book are the 1920s, the conditions suggest a much earlier date due to the setting in a remote hill area where change is much slower than in the more densely populated and more accessible areas. Such conditions can aggravate the situation for the very much lower level of income means there is a cautious approach in accepting change which, if not successful, can result at the best in the loss of years of work and at worst, bankruptcy.

A recently married young couple were lucky enough to be able to rent a farm—they pooled their resources and took the plunge. Take into account that the first rent will be due in six months and will have to come out of the cash for essentials—animals, machinery, tools and furniture—as it is not possible to make any appreciable amount of money in such a short space of time. It might have been possible to borrow a work horse, if one of the couple came from a line of established farmers, whilst wedding presents may include a few laying hens and, if very lucky, maybe a goose and gander. Even so there would be no income for nine months at the earliest, so sheep were the best buy. Indeed, on hill land in this part of Wales you had to have sheep, hardy hill sheep, and anyone who did not have a good and comprehensive knowledge of them had best keep their distance! But in Summer, wedding time, the only way to buy them is as ewes and lambs, but there again that is the most expensive time. So machinery and equipment has to be kept absolutely to a minimum to leave as much cash as possible to purchase animals, and probably only amounted to a two horse mower, a horse rake, gambo or cart, a

A tipping cart

tipping cart, plough, set of tooth harrows (or scuffle if you were going to grow potatoes or turnips).

From this sort of a beginning it took at least five years to get established and another five to get to the stage where improvements or up-dating could be considered. As things stood, money could not be borrowed because of the depressed state of farming.

A huge amount has been written about farms and farmers, some of it by people who don't mean any harm but more often by farmers themselves in a facetious or tongue-in-cheek joking attitude almost as if to demean themselves and their occupation. Like all other people and occupations, to attempt to typify is to destroy.

Farmers include all types, much the same as will be found in any other walk of life—the satisfied, the grumbler, the pessimist and the optimist. I have known the outright miserable, not necessarily a bad farmer, but not the best of neighbours to meet for a chat on a Sunday morning. More often than not there is a certain amount of individuality engendered by isolation and the need to make decisions and take action in what is often described as the drop of the hat.

To our city friends who have been fed with the idea of the straw chewing, welli-shod, hole in the hat individual, I would say that this type certainly exists and is often the subject of the farmers' jokes about themselves. They enjoy them, so why not you. But they are an endangered species and likely to become extinct in the very near future, mostly due to modern education and greater expectations. Whilst the urban person is often a very skilled person in a specific area and has only to rely on that skill for the greater part of his or her life, the farmer has to be a 'Jack of all Trades' not out of choice, but from necessity. From the moment he wakes until he goes to sleep all his senses are in operation so as to cope with a kaleidoscope of conditions and circumstances, be they due to family, weather or animals, mostly known and usual, but with the unexpected to give a little spice to life! He needs to be physically strong to tackle the work, often at a time when most folks would head for cover. He may not have the choice, the comfort of his animals being more important than his own. He may often have to go to the limit of his strength and endurance as his future success may depend on it.

'Patience is a virtue' says the old adage. With farmers it is a must when it takes as much as three years for the proof of a cattle breeding programme to be demonstrated. Patience is only superseded by the farmer's wife, who has to have complete faith in what her man is doing. In no way do they have to be 'Super' people but it would help.

Biased? Of course! It wouldn't be natural if it were otherwise. Be that as it may, it is hard to find any other calling where such a variety of capabilities are called for. It is not to say that professional people like doctors, dentists or managers don't have greater skills; they may have, but in a different way entirely and far more specialised.

First and foremost the farmer must be a good businessman with an aptitude for figures—not farmers' daughters (although that may have a distinct bearing on his success in the future)—it is the arithmetic variety that is paramount. He must be a good judge of people, including farmers' daughters! A great asset is the ability to look surprised, to register disbelief, or appear not interested—a great help in closing a deal to his own advantage. But most of all he must be a good judge of an animal and its potential. It goes without saying that he must also be honest—to be anything else would mean loss of trust by the neighbours and shortage of customers and friends. In an industry that has to rely on everyone involved in the business, that would be nothing short of disaster.

Over the years a code of behaviour has evolved, unwritten, but none the less binding for all that, and anyone who does or will not abide by it is likely to 'get a rough ride'. Animals stray, lose their markings, cause damage to neighbours hedges or crops, and all these events require fair dealing or return without question. Such things as law courts are unnecessary and costly and no law can replace goodwill and understanding, indeed they only succeed in antagonising and destroying the people involved, the only gain being to the legal profession. The local saying is 'Let dogs delight to bark and bite, but leave the law alone'—good advice to all as well as the farming fraternity.

Another great asset is a level head and a good temper so as to cope with a job which at times can be frustrating in the extreme, and nobody, and I mean nobody, can ever hope to be a success with animals if he loses his temper, especially when training them.

The wife has to be an out-going person, a mother to child, man and beast! Also a good worker and often, and most importantly, a good and sympathetic listener—a cut knee, a bad loss, bad news, a death in the family—she has to listen, sympathise and console, she knows that the best cure for the knee is a kiss on the cheek and a cup of tea, and that a sympathetic ear soothes even the most awful situations. A tower of strength, unseen, unheard, unsung, but always there to fall back on, worth more than 'all the tea in China'.

Often, when we talk of years ago and about our predecessors, the general inference is that they were not up to date. Science has taken great strides and we have been fortunate in being able to take advantage. However, in those past years, better use was made of what was available than is the case today. Often the conditions, tools, machinery and in particular, capital, simply were not to be had, and improvisation took over with the use of whatever was available. In those days only the more fortunate were able to read and write and had a limited knowledge of arithmetic. Even so, this was not such a drawback as is often imagined—buildings were built (and fine ones to boot), roads made, cloth woven and food grown and processed without any pen and paper being used.

One instance I recall in the late twenties was the local handyman carpenter. Although he had no schooling as a boy, he had taught himself to read in a small way, and though he could not add anything more difficult than twos and fours, he built timber and corrugated French and Dutch barns with tools that today's carpenters would scorn. Twelve poles were necessary, six beams and roof trusses, five ridge pieces, ten eaves pieces and twenty-four diagonals for stability. These were all felled in the larch plantation, cut to length and notched to fit. The only tools that were used were saw and axe, with taught string used to give straight lines and a two-foot rule for measurements. Then the timber was taken to the site for erection. The holes were dug to receive the upright poles on a field with a slight slope and when those poles were in the right places and vertical they were all the same height.

Simple? It may be with modern equipment, but not when I tell you that the only levelling device was a bottle filled with water until there was only a small bubble of air? One side of the bottle had a scratch mark from the base to the neck, which was the 'Top'. Two marks crossed this line, marks arrived at by placing the bottle on a relatively level surface and marking the lower end of the bubble, then turning the bottle one hundred and eighty degrees and marking again. When the bubble was centred between these two marks the surface on which it rested was level.

Great changes have taken place in the words used and in the language itself. A lot of this is due to the effect of schooling, but the greatest influence has been the ability to travel further and more often than our parents and grandparents could. Before the motor car many people spent their whole lives in the county, even in just their own parish. As walking was the only means of travel, the chance of marriage between couples further apart than the distance they could walk was unlikely. One exception to this general rule was the farm lads who were hired for the year by a farmer at the Hiring Fair in May. They might just might be lucky enough to find favour with a lass in the area.

It followed that outside influences took quite a while to filter through, but this all changed with the coming of the bicycle, the motor cycle and eventually the car with a steadily increasing tempo. As a result the semi-closed and tightly knit communities were completely fragmented and the family and neighbourhood esprit-de-corps destroyed. This had both advantages and disadvantages. Whilst it did away with the old prejudices, it destroyed the trust that existed between the people of the area. It also did away with the authoritarian position of the so-called black hat brigade, who kept the locals in line with their their somewhat limited ideas of morality and the like. Deacons and church elders tended to rule the local people moralwise, not always correctly, but in line with their personal opinions and sometimes to their personal advantage. Contact with outside influences diminished people's credulity and, in consequence, the authority of the church elders, with the result that eventually they ceased to have any control over the people. Sadly, this contributed to the decline of the church and chapel attendance. The time when everyone looked 'over the hedge' to see how his neighbour was getting on ended, and the 'look after yourself' syndrome took over to the great disadvantage of local communities.

Wireless brought the wider world to the remotest household in a positive manner, opposing the usual vague and biased views of the national press, often to the confusion of the listener—many of the country people were surprised and not a little put out to find that the political party for which they had been voting stood for the opposite views than those for which they thought they had voted!

*   *   *   *   *

The farmer's year is not a specified number of weeks or days—his is a cycle of time and seasons, but no two seasons are the same. They may be earlier or later than normal, if indeed there is such a thing as normal—normal tending to be the exception rather than the rule. Harvest time can drift by a month between one year and the next.

No two years are the same, no two farmers are the same, and the difference in farms is endless—hill, moorland, fertile lowland and any combination, and each factor has a bearing on the type of farming favoured by the occupying farmer. The only harvest that normally starts on a firm date is that of the hop, and that is only grown on a very small percentage of farms as it requires soil with specific qualities. With this uncertainty it is hard to say when the farming year starts and ends and it may be best to use the calendar year.

Generally the farming at the beginning of the year is low key and consists mainly of keeping the animals comfortable and happy. A typical day would mean being out of bed at seven to half past and off to the cowhouses to see that all is well, then to the horses if it is a 'one man farm'. If a waggoner is hired, or maybe a son is old enough, the horses would be their responsibility and like the cattle would be fed and watered before breakfast. Often the mornings would be cold and damp or the ground covered with snow, but it was always dark, so the work had to be done with a paraffin lamp. Feeding done, one or two very hungry men would hurry to the house where breakfast was ready on the table.

Breakfast over, it was off to suckle the calves and milk off the surplus milk. As this time approaches the cows' body clocks and the

48

calves' stomachs tell them so, and the noise is deafening—cows calling for their calves and the calves answering. But there is a sudden hush as the doors between the two are opened and then a concerted rush for the desired teats, followed by delicious sucking sounds indicating the relish of what the cow has on offer. When each has had what is considered a good feed it is taken from the cow and with much physical resistance returned to its pen, and the process repeated until all are back in their pens—each looking at the door with an 'It just isn't fair, there's plenty there yet' expression on their faces. The surplus that the calves do not need, indeed which, if they were allowed to take, could cause them harm, is milked off by hand, ('They'll never make a machine to milk a cow—anyway no self-respecting cow would let a machine have any milk!')

But why is it that the cow in the cow house has too much milk for its calf and the cow out in the field does not? It's a fine example mother nature. The cow in the field has, as we say, the calf at foot. When the calf is just born it takes only as much as it needs and like any good baby goes to sleep until its tummy wakes it up again whereupon mother is there to supply the necessary. As the calf does not take all of the mother's milk the amount of milk produced is reduced according to the amount left in the cow's udder, and so a balance is achieved between supply and demand. As the calf grows and needs more it continues to suck and to 'boont'—to thump its mother's udder with its head. That signals to the cow and mother nature that more milk is required to cope with the growing appetite, so more milk is produced by the cow, but only for so long. Gradually the milk supply diminishes and the young animal now finds it necessary to feed itself by grazing, and the weaning process begins.

To encourage a cow to produce more milk you empty the udder completely. This explains how you encourage more than the calf needs, a sort of exploitation it is true, but the sort that does no harm to anyone. No doubt the learned could explain it in more technical terms, but being the one with mud on my boots that is the best I can offer.

At this time of the year milking is done by the cowman and the milk taken to the house to be skimmed or separated by the housewife. If a separator is a part of the dairy equipment, the milk is placed in it still warm and the cream separated from the milk. If there is no separator, the milk is placed in leads, or large shallow pans, where it was allowed to cool, the cream rising to the surface as it does so, in the same way that the cream rises to the neck of the bottle of the daily pint bottle. (This is less evident with today's homogenised milk.)

In summer, the housewife does the milking to let the man get on with harvesting or other outside work demanding his immediate attention.

Milking done, the cows are let out to water and, if the weather is reasonable, are taken to the winter pasture, except for the newly calved or the particularly good milker which are put back in the 'Beast house', the local name for the cowhouse.

While the cowhouse is empty the 'Mexing' is done—the cleaning out from the cows' overnight stay. Fresh bedding is put on the 'stand', the raised portion of the cowhouse, to keep the animals clean and comfortable. The cows to be kept in are then allowed back and the second feed of the day, or second foddering, is given.

The young stock come next, except the young calves, which had been let out of their pens for water and arrive back to find a rack, or 'cratch', filled with hay or oats as the case may be, and a good spread of bracken for them to lie on when their bellies were full. The sucking calves have their water carried for them, and it is amazing to see how much they will drink at this age, almost as though they take advantage of the fact that it has to be carried!

By now the separating had been done, and skimmed milk with a supplement would be ready for the bucket-reared calf or calves. This was a way of increasing the number of young cattle for sale without having to keep an extra cow and would also make use of the surplus skimmed milk. If possible these calves were bought early in the year so as to be well on their way by the time that young pigs were purchased and needed the milk. These pigs would take all the milk left over until they were killed for bacon.

Bucket calves were trained to drink milk from the bucket by allowing the calf to suck ones fingers dipped in milk. While they sucked, the hand was slowly lowered into the bucket, and when slightly lower than the surface the fingers would be spread so that by sucking the calf drew milk though the gap. Then gradually the fingers were withdrawn and hopefully the calf went on sucking. Several feeds were necessary before the calf learned to put its head in the bucket and drink without a little enticement. The calf also learnt that to obtain the last drop, it had to pick up the bucket by its rim and tilt the bucket so that the milk ran into its mouth.

Then came the turn of the sheep. At this time of year they were kept in a field or fields not too far from the house, and during the previous summer a stack of hay had been placed convenient to these fields to make feeding easier. Racks were placed side by side as near to the stack as possible and hay was sliced from the stack and carried and put in the racks. A critical and experienced eye surveyed the flock noting any late in coming for its feed, and deciding if any action was called for according to the symptoms displayed, whether now or in the near future.

Assuming all was well, you proceeded to the next job—likely to be hedging at this time of the year, but there was no fixed programme. This was the time of day that was subject to need or maybe chance: cows may need to be taken for service; an animal has strayed or is sick or is dead; a gate might require mending. If the weather was bad, there was threshing to be done with the resulting winnowing. Often yesterday's plans became tomorrow's, not from a change of mind but due to circumstances beyond one's control. Quite often there was a clash of priorities, one good for the short term, another better in the long, a case of 'Decisions, Decisions'. Usually experience came to bear and the clash was only momentary.

Whatever course was taken, the time would be filled until dinner time. This would be ready on time and last as long as it took to eat it, then it was off to give the youngest calves their midday suck. This was followed by a feed for the cattle and away to the next chosen job which had to end before darkness fell and animals had to be let out again for water and given a further feed, and the cattle brought home from the field to be housed for the night.

It was tea-time by now and too dark to do anything more without a light. Tea could be taken a little more leisurely than dinner. So, maybe turn around to the fire for a few minutes, out comes the old pipe, dark from use and scorched a little around the top of the bowl. (It is not the same pipe as used after Chapel on Sunday—that is kept specially and is 'Not so nice a smoke as the 'old 'un.') Then the night's suckling of the calves, young and older, and again silence is restored.

A final feed, check up, everyone eating, all comfortable, before a few minutes were spent contemplating their contentment, a feeling of happiness and hope for the future, tempered with the thought and almost a wish that your own wants and wishes were no more complicated than theirs.

So, a winter's day almost comes to an end. A good day? A bad day? Or an average day? They all have their turn, hopefully the bad days will be in a great minority. Today was a good one, and so to supper and bed. Supper was taken around nine o'clock, and afterwards it was sit with feet on the old fender, shoes off, pipe lit with a coal from the fire. A final browse through the Mid Wales Independent section of the *Wellington Journal and Shrewsbury News* and, last of all before going to bed, wind the old Grandfather clock, a clicking, clacking sound, and Grandfather is left in charge until he strikes seven in the morning.

Every day on the farm is unique, so is every week and season. Priorities alter, weather changes—all as predictable as the flight of the butterfly. But gradually Spring would approach, the time of planting, of lambing, of hopes.

Spring doesn't start on March 21st, but when things spring, a trite statement maybe, but true. Buds start to show, grass greens up, blackbirds find a place to nest and sit on some high place to sing about it, but, most important to the farmer, the soil dries and begins to warm up. Seed sowing becomes possible and the lambs start to arrive.

When the lambs come they take priority over everything, even the farmer and his family. They represent success or failure, and for a whole month a day has twenty-four hours whether you like it or not! If a ewe or lamb needs attention they get it. Sleep is a luxury, grabbed when the opportunity occurs and the ability to fall asleep at the drop of a hat becomes a habit. The daily round of feeding and tending the cattle and calves has to become more flexible and fitted in but in no way are they neglected.

A glance at the flock and any ewe due to lamb is seen and recognised and memorised for surveillance later. Any in the process of lambing is helped to give birth, and if there are complications they have to be dealt with in such a way as to cause as little distress as possible and ensure a trouble free future for both ewe and lamb, or lambs, as the case may be. Occasionally, after a difficult birth, the ewe and her offspring have to be taken into the shelter of the barn or some place prepared for the eventuality, and if necessary the lambs have to be fed with cows' milk until the ewe has recovered sufficiently to provide the lamb with her own. This is mostly the job of the housewife, or the children if they are old enough. Similarly, any lamb that is weakly or starved is taken poste-haste to the house, fed (sometimes a couple of drops of brandy would be added to the milk from the same bottle as used the previous year!) and wrapped in a piece of old blanket or something similar and placed near the fire where it is not too hot. To try to warm a starved lamb too quickly would only hasten its end so a little patience is required. When it begins to warm up it will normally call for its mother signalling that it is alright. But, if after a little while it gives a weak bleat, slowly dying away, a hopeless despairing note, the chances of recovery are small if any. As they say, you cannot win them all, so away to see to the others, and better luck next time.

This is also the time for sowing the corn. Spring wheat was sown, for winter wheat stood very little chance of survival here—the heavy clay-based soil becomes waterlogged in the long wet days of winter and the seed is totally drowned. If there should be a few fine dry days in February and a fairly light seedbed, the opportunity would be used to plant the wheat as wheat is slow to mature and it gave a better crop, but this was the exception rather than the rule.

Ploughing went on apace. That is if you can describe two horses pulling a single furrow as such. The waggoner started feeding his team at 6 a.m. and kept them eating until 8. The feed was oat sheaves chopped into one inch lengths with the head included and if an extra demand was to be made due to pressure of work then extra oats were added. The chaff was cut after dark the preceding day by the light of a paraffin lamp, and soaked in a tub. This softened the straw and swelled the grain to make it easier to eat, so

A plough

53

saving feeding time and making it easier to digest. In this way it benefited the horse in much the same way that glucose is more beneficial to the athlete than plain sugar.

If the farm was a one man farm the sheep due to lamb were put in a field adjoining the field being ploughed so that the ploughman-shepherd could do both jobs at once. If one of the ewes was likely to need attention he could keep an eye on her and at the appropriate moment tether the horses and go to the rescue.

The team was always addressed as 'boys' or 'lads', in the masculine, whereas cars or tractors nowadays are referred to in the feminine. Why, I don't know. Often very few directions were necessary as a practiced team knew exactly what was required of them. For instance, when ploughing one of the team walked in the furrow and automatically turned into the furrow to start a new one, the only thing required was to ensure the horses walked a sufficiently wide circle to make the plough arrive in the correct place at the beginning of a 'new' furrow, in much the same way as a car has to be steered a little wide during a tight turn to get the back wheels in the right place.

If the area to be ploughed is sixty yards wide it will be measured and marked for two 'cops', each cop ten yards from the outsides with forty yards between, the reason being that when ten yards on each side of each cop was ploughed there would be an area twenty yards between of unploughed land, the land that was ploughed both sides of the cop was ploughed travelling in a clockwise direction and called 'gathering' whereas the rest was ploughed anti-clockwise termed 'slitting', the reason being that at no time was the travelling on the headlands at the top and bottom of the field in excess of twenty yards. It follows, of course, that a change of direction takes place when changing from gathering to slitting and when that moment arrives word-of-mouth commands have to be reinforced by the use of the 'lines'.

But first the cop has to be made. Sticks or pegs were used to mark out the line, for the straighter the resulting cop, the higher the ploughman was rated. In the process the horses had to do what is practically an about turn when the end of the first 'trig' (the first furrow about half the size of the usual) was reached. The vocal command 'Zic' or 'Zee right back lads'—a command to do an about turn in a clock-wise direction—was given and accompanied with the necessary control with the lines.

'Whoa' was the usual command to stop and I think fairly universal so needs no elaboration. The next command to get the team moving again was 'Together lads' or maybe 'Now my lads TOGETHER' if a special effort was wanted. When the gathering widened, the turn became more or less a right angle at the end of the furrow and the verbal order was shortened to 'Zic Back' or 'Zee Back', which then had to be used twice at both ends to complete a 180° turn to set the team back down the field.

Seat yourself on the grass at the top end of a sloping field that gets progressively steeper. The time is April, sowing time. The field has been ploughed earlier and this morning the farmer sowed the corn—wheat, barley or oats. The corn was taken to the field in sacks and placed on the bare furrow. The 'Sower goes forth to sow' and filling a hopper with the corn from the sack he hangs it on a strap over his shoulder, the hopper being a kidney-shaped container with a vertical handle held by the left hand while the right is used to 'sow' the grain. As the sower's left foot comes forward a handful of grain is taken from the hopper and as the right foot comes forward the grain is thrown forward and upwards in a crescent-shaped arc to fall evenly over the ground between the track travelled before and where his next track will be, adjusting his action to account for the direction of the wind. A very similar system was used for artificial manures and grass seeds but the size of the handful and width of the 'cast' was varied according to the crop or manure.

With the seed and then the manure in place they have to be harrowed in, so the team is hooked to the harrows—two iron frames with six inch spikes sticking down, hooked to a wooden bar about six feet long so that the two frames are dragged side by side along the furrows to break up the soil and cover the seed and the manure. As you watch from your vantage point, gradually man and horses disappear to view as they go over the bank onto the steeper slope, first the feet and legs and as they progress, the bodies and last to be seen is the farmer's hat bobbing rhythmically. The dogs, Turk and Nell, curled up nearby show signs of life; Turk gets up and looks to see if he can see his master, can not, but probably hears the sounds of the horses, so does a turn as dogs do and lies down again. Nell opens one eye, sees what Turk is doing and when Turk lies down again shuts it and returns to dozing. Slowly and in perfect rhythm the heads of the team reappear, the farmer's head between them, until all is in full view once again, the legs of the man in a small cloud of dust that rises as the harrows disturb the drying soil.

Dinner time comes and the horses are unhooked and taken back to the stable, the gears or harness taken off and put on the pegs driven into the walls for the purpose, the horses then let out to drink and a feed of soaked chaff placed ready in the manger for when they come back in. This was timed as near as possible to be at 12 noon, but as with a lot of other things on the farm was subject to variation. Maybe the job that was being done was finished before twelve or took until half past to finish, then time has to take second place, the job takes first.

Next come the cattle, to water, feed and clean (mex out), the second feed for the horses then dinner at 1 o'clock.

Dinner over, it is out to finish any job necessary with the cows then 'gear up' and back to the plough and the sheep until time to unhook and get the sheep and cattle fixed for the night—horses fed and watered, cows the same and any sheep or lambs needing attention dealt with. It is a rather tired man who sits down to tea at 5 o'clock.

Then comes time for a smoke and out to the routine milking, suckling, and feeding, cutting and mixing chaff for tomorrow. See that all is right with the sheep, now in a field close to the house for supervision overnight. Bed about 10, but up to have a look around about 12 to 1 o'clock. If all is serene, with no sign of any ewe thinking of lambing, it is back to bed until 6, when the whole thing starts again.

If there has been a hard frost overnight the soil would be frozen and ploughing impossible, so instead the time is used to get the farmyard manure out on the field. The horses are geared up, the Shafter in the cart gears and the Leader in the long gears, hooked up and the cart filled with dung forks, to be filled up and heaped like the roof of a house. Once taken to the field, with a bumping and banging of iron tyres over rough stone roads, the cart is tilted slightly and a heap pulled out on to the ground with the dung hook (pronounced dunuck). The cart is then moved on five or six yards and the operation repeated and so on till the cart is empty. Then back for more, until time or muck ran out.

If that happened, there was always hedging, or pleaching, to do. There are two methods, one uses stakes whilst the other, crop and pleach, makes use of any growing wood that is available. In this system, stems or trunks are cut off at hedge height and so form a living support for the sticks that are pleached. Pleaching involves selecting suitable living wood which is then cut in a slanting manner near its base. When the base of the wedge shape piece is thin it is slit down a short distance and then the stick is bent away from the cut and along the hedge, woven between the uprights. Dead wood is used to fill any gaps, so as to make the hedge stockproof and also to protect the young shoots from grazing animals. It sounds simple enough, but no two sticks or two hedges are the same, so beware if you have a notion to try.

An enormous amount of change has taken place in methods and of course machines since the 1920s. The Great War, so-called, gave a certain impetus to agriculture, but the following years were dominated by an economic theory that trade with other countries was more important than production of farm produce at home. Foodstuffs were imported in return for our manufactured goods. This was followed by the depression of the late 20s and early 30s which nearly bankrupted both industry and farming and the result was a period of stagnation.

Some of the tools and machines we had were pleasant to use on account of the completeness, peace, and untroubled atmosphere that they gave rise to, but others were difficult and disagreeable and in some cases downright unpleasant.

You may not agree that a scythe and a sickle are machines, but the fact that they were powered by a man, (or woman for that matter, as many women on the farms could and did use them) does not make them anything but machines in my mind. Until the advent of the horse-drawn mower the scythe was the only means of mowing grass for haymaking, and was also used for cutting barley and oat crops, and sometimes the wheat. The scythe, clumsy as it may seem, and is to the novice, is hugely adept at cutting off plants at ground level. It was very heavy work, especially if the crop was good, but at least there was the satisfaction of growing a good crop with the likelihood of plenty of hay for the stock for the next winter.

The swathe cut was about three feet six inches wide and so quite a bulky row of grass resulted, for as the grass was cut it was carried away with the swing of the scythe and deposited on the ground that had been cut to make the previous swathe. In this way it was certain that there was no grass left uncut. This swathe was too bulky and heavy to harvest and so the pikel (a long pitchfork with two tines) was brought into play, for the grass had to be 'tedded', that is

Turning the hay by hand on my grandparents' farm

shaken out and spread as thinly on the ground as conditions permitted so as to hasten the drying process.

The following day, all being well, the hand rake was used to turn the hay, by now smelling beautiful—no other scent can compare, even those made in France. As with most tools, there is a knack in using the hay rake. The teeth, as with a garden rake, are at right angles to the handle, but unlike the garden rake must not dig into the soil, so the handle has to be kept high—as a child I was told to 'Keep 'is 'ead up'. The rake is put forward as far as it can usefully be and dropped to the ground, pulled towards you but not lifting it for a little distance, about a foot or a little more, then lifted and the speed of the pull increased so that the hay drops off the rake on to the ground with the underside on top. So off you went down one row, then changed hands and returned. May your thumbs never get sore!

Luck holding, the next day would be fine, you would tedd again or more usually row up for 'cocking'. This could be done in three ways—with hand rakes, horse rake or occasionally a 'tumbler'. This latter was the forerunner of the hay sweep used with tractors, and collected hay on the same principle, but with the sweep the tractor was reversed, leaving the hay to slide off the tines. With horses this was not possible. Imagine a wooden contraption having a vertical frame and, pointing forward on the ground, a number of 'tines' some four feet long and tapering to a point. I wonder now if they

A tumbler

had iron tips, but I cannot be sure. Fitted to the upper edge of the vertical frame was an identical set of tines pointing backwards in a horizontal position, giving a side view of a square letter Z. This whole had a spindle arrangement to which the horse was attached, and here my memory becomes somewhat vague. The horse was driven with the lines, the operator walking behind, and the tines slid along the ground. The hay collected on the tines, and—wait for it—the driver grasps two of the rear facing tines, lifts them up, the forward tines stick in the soil and the whole machine rotates on the cross spindle and settles down after a half turn, rolling over the hay already gathered. What were the upper, back-facing tines are now ready to gather the next bit of hay. This assumes that the driver managed to keep his lines from getting entangled in the turning-over process. The problem with this method was that there was quite a wide area between the tipping and the start of the next gathering, so that a hand rake would be used to 'close up' the row to avoid waste and loss of time when cocking.

The horse rake was a more efficient means of rowing up, but unlike the tumbler had to be bought rather than made. It was a two wheeled vehicle, fitted with shafts for hooking up to the horse, and better still as far as the man was concerned, it had a seat! This was an old man's job and the envy of the onlooker who was stuck with a pikel. The rake was fitted with steel tines, curved in a circular fashion carried at such a height as to be close to the ground. When pulled forward by the horse it collected the hay in the curve of the tines. When sufficient hay had been gathered the tines were lifted up and out of the hay which was left in a nicely packed roll. This continued across the field and then returned, dropping the rolls opposite the ones from the previous turn. In this way the whole field would be 'rowed up' and ready for cocking.

The third, slowest and most laborious method was the hand rake and this was only used when no other means was available, mostly on small farms where it was considered uneconomic to buy machinery on account of the small acreage to be dealt with. This way the hay is raked from both sides to form a row, choosing the necessary width to collect a suitable amount for the row.

To anyone seeing a field of hay in cocks, a rare sight now-a-days, it appears like a lot of symmetrical heaps of hay shaped like pudding basins turned upside down.

One must realise that there was no such a thing as a baler, round, square or any other shape; the hay was loose and had to be handled in this state. It follows that if these cocks of hay were just heaps pushed together haphazardly, then when it came to gathering it with a pikel to put on a cart it would be just a woolly mess with endless time wasted in gathering it up as well as being almost impossible to build into a decent load. Also, if the cocks were not properly formed they would be saturated in even a light shower of rain and all the work done previously would be wasted. So when starting to make a cock, a suitably sized base was made and built up layer upon layer in as flat wads as it was possible to get, each layer slightly smaller than the previous one. Finally a cap formed of hay was put on to give it an all over cover in case it should rain. But when the time came to haul the hay to the rick or barn the layers would have flattened and firmed making it easy to 'pitch', that is to get it on the pikel and put it up to the person making the load.

Cocking the hay was usually done by the womenfolk and any children who were capable of using a pikel and who would be rewarded by a taste of cider if such luxuries could be afforded. I was one of these children and I enjoyed doing it, knowing that it was for the good of my parents. I was never expected to do anything beyond my capabilities or put in any danger, unless you can call riding on an empty gambo on a rough road dangerous.

The gambo was a two-wheeled conveyance or carriage with shafts for the horse to be 'hucked up', hooked up. The shafts continued for a further 8 or 9 feet behind the horse and this part was boarded to form a platform with a rail-like arrangement to stop the load fouling the wheels, and with vertical staves at each corner so as to stabilise any load. The knack of loading it was to keep the

A gambo/cart—when without the sides it is a gambo

corners highest and the sides a little higher than the middle but at the same time keeping the whole uniform and firm. Simple you say. Simple if every pikelful of hay was the same amount, the same sort of hay, and came up to you on the load in the same place. Simple if you had all the time in the world and didn't have to keep working while the gambo was moving to get ready for the next lot! And the field may be on a slope. With the load finally ready to take home, ropes were slung over and tied to a ring on one side of the gambo and pulled down and tied on the other side. If a bad road had to be traversed or a steep field to be crossed the harvest knot was used. This was an arrangement with a pulley block action that defies description. I even doubt whether I could make one myself now, but it certainly made for a very tight tie down. It was not used as a general rule as friction in the tightening always fell more or less in the same place and caused wear and weakening of the rope and shortened its life.

The load was then taken to its designated storing place, be it barn or rick, generally referred to as a stack. The custom was for the person who loaded the hay to have the job of unloading it. As a badly loaded load is hard to unload, it behove the loader to do a systematic job to help him or herself later. Meanwhile the pitcher on the field became the builder of the stack or the 'mye', using the same techniques as for loading the gambo.

As the stack grew it tended to become unstable and 'props' were stood at the sides to take the weight and to make sure that the stack shrunk evenly under its own weight. The sides and the ends were made to over-hang slightly to avoid wetting from rain. At what is considered the right time a sloping roof was made with the ridge as keen as the material would allow. When consolidated naturally, the stack would be thatched when time and opportunity permitted, usually after the corn harvest.

With a mower, one man and a pair of horses could mow as much as four men with scythes, with a further advantage that the grass was left in a much thinner swathe so did not require as much tedding. But the process was similar from there on.

There was quite a lot of opposition to the mower by some of the older farmers. Their reasons were many and varied such as: it would ruin a good team of horses; it would kill the best grasses and let the poor stuff grow; and such statements as: it's a lazy man's job; you'll just sit on a seat and work the poor horses to death. One particularly wet harvest was even blamed on 'them new-fangled machines upsetting the weather'—this was in 1926 when there were only 26 completely dry days in the whole year!

A deliverer in action on my grandparents' farm

A hay mower posing for a photograph

Every year one hopes to get the hay harvest cleared up before the corn is ripe, otherwise both have to be run together and then one has to suffer on account of the other. It is a hazard that has to be accepted and can happen after a late spring or wet summer, quite common in this high rainfall area. Not a great acreage of corn was grown, for the soil is often thin on a clay base which in wet weather gets waterlogged which the corn plant will not tolerate. Alternatively the fields have a rocky base on which the soil is often poor and thin.

For corn, as with grass, the scythe was an important machine together with the sickle. The scythe was used on its own, but the sickle was used with a curved stick wielded in the left hand and the sickle in the right, generally referred to as 'The Hook and The Crook.' The crook was held in such a way as to catch the head of the wheat when it fell after being cut with the hook, this way there was no danger of any of the heads of corn being cut off by the sickle at the end of its stroke, and seeing that this made the bread for the following year was very important indeed.

If a scythe was used, cutting off the head was avoided by cutting into the 'live'. Instead of the corn being cut and carried by the scythe on to the space already cut, as with hay, the cut was made the other way, into the standing corn. This way the standing corn held up the head of the cut corn and avoided loss, but this method required a very experienced wielder to cut the swathe 'clean'. With oats and barley the weight of the head did not pose this problem, neither was the crop of such prime importance, so these crops were cut on to the space cleared by the previous cut. Where the hook and crook were used the user collected sufficient corn which was handed to the person tying up, and not placed on the ground until it was tied up. In this way not a single straw was dropped. One other precaution used to preserve every grain was the method of tying— only four straws for a band placed around the centre with their heads left dangling out in the open so that they dried quickly should it rain.

Sometimes the man tying up the sheaves gathered the cut corn up in his arms until he had collected enough for a sheaf and then passed a band of straw around the sheaf, then twisted the ends together before tucking them under itself in such a way as to tighten the band—to tuck it under the wrong way would leave the sheaf slackly tied. More often the sheaves were formed by a man using a pikel, and another doing the tying up.

An improvement came with the 'Self Deliverer', a similar cutting arrangement to the mower, but having a platform fixed behind the cutting knife which carried the cut corn until swept off by a system of mechanical rakes, sometimes referred to as sails, leaving the sheaves ready for tying. This was capable of cutting much faster than the scythe and at the same time releasing more people for the tying up, so greatly speeding up the process.

When tied up the sheaf has to be 'stuck' a job that looks so simple and yet those of an inexperienced sticker fall over whereas the others stay up! As a farmer once told James Herriot, 'It isn't what you do, it's how you do it' and was actually referring to sticking corn when he said it!

Occasionally, when there was a very bad spell of weather, the sheaves in the stuckles got soaked under the bands and there seemed to be no chance of drying them. Desperate measures had to be adopted. The stuckles were taken apart and the bands cut, enough to break the heart of any man but nevertheless it had to be done. Then a light band was tied near the top of a pair and stood up again in the form of an umbrella on a fresh patch of land. If lucky and the wet part dried a 'double' band, that is two lengths of straw twisted together, was used to tie two sheaves in one. Then the upper band was taken away and, due to the size of the double sheaf,

A self-deliverer in travelling mode

it would stand on its own and given the chance would dry out. This method was called 'Styching' and the umbrella formed a 'Styche'.

If the harvested hay or corn was nice and dry, the larger the square stack or round rick the better. If there was any doubt as to the dryness, the stacks were small and narrow to avoid excessive fermentation and over heating, the cause of many a farm fire, also to allow air contact to as large an area as possible.

Loading the corn onto the gambo was very much the same as for hay. After the base of the load was built, the loader then laid the sheaves with the heads toward the middle of the load placing them side by side and progressing in a clockwise direction, keeping the middle of the load slightly below the outside edge, and filling it with an occasional sheaf as the occasion demanded to maintain a correct level. When a suitable quantity was on the gambo, the middle was filled over the level, sheaves were placed lengthways where the rope would cross, the ropes tied down and the load taken away.

In the case of a stack being built at the side of a field or in an uncovered position, a 'base' was needed to keep the crop from getting damp. Branches of wood were placed over the projected base area and then covered with litter or other expendable material. Only the latter would be required in a barn with a dry floor. A stuckle was set up at the centre of the area to be used, then a circle of sheaves was laid with their heads resting on this stuckle, and so on making the required shape.

Then the same circular system of laying was carried out, ensuring that the outer ends of the sheaves must (and this is vital) droop to make sure that any rain driven by the wind will drop off and not run along the straw into the centre of the rick itself.

In a barn this was not a hazard, but the same method was used to avoid any contact between the head and the floor. As with the rick the building up was done in a clockwise direction, with the base, then the inside rings worked to the outside, and thereafter working inward from the outside ring until the middle was covered, each succeeding ring covering the head of the previous one until the barn was filled or there was no more corn available.

If there was a barn on the farm, the wheat was always stored in it. If not, it was put in ricks, each containing about two gambo loads. A small rick could be threshed in a day, the rest of the crop being left undisturbed until such time as it could be dealt with.

All the corn in ricks and stacks had to be thatched to make them weatherproof and avoid waste. The corn ricks were first given a cover of coarse grass or short rushes which was then 'peaked' up with the same sort of material to give a nice clean ridge for the thatch. The threshed wheat straw was sometimes used but more often than not common rushes or so-called candle rushes were used.

Thatching and thatchers are becoming scarce, so a description of the art may not be out of place. Rushes of suitable length were selected and cut with the scythe, tied in bundles or sheaves and hauled to the rick to be thatched. These bundles were stacked in such a way as to make them 'heat' and become pliable and lie much closer together and so be more effective as thatch. Pegs would have been made from hazel sticks or saved from last year's thatching, and boonds made or, if times were good, thatching cord purchased from the local grocer, to wit Pugh's the Shop.

Starting on the right-hand edge of the roof a line of pegs, (eighteen inches to two feet in length) were placed horizontally, each having a ball of string with the one end tied to it with a slip knot, and each ball of a length somewhat longer than the roof of the stack, to allow for fastening to other pegs used in the thatching. A ladder was placed about eighteen inches away from these pegs (and the edge of the roof) in order to begin laying the rushes. A bundle of rushes placed on the left of the thatcher was kept from falling off by a pikel stuck in the roof by his side.

A handful of rushes was taken, combed with the fingers and laid on the lower peg, then another handful close to it nearer to the ladder, and so on until there was one layer from the peg to the ladder.

Another layer goes on above this, covering about half of the previous layer and so on up the roof until the ridge is reached where a few longer rushes are chosen that will cover the top. Pegs are now pushed into the stack in line with the pegs placed at the start and the strings brought across and tied to the newly inserted pegs with a thatcher's knot, which resembles a 'rabbit knot', a country name for a 'Clove hitch'. Two musts here. The rushes must be padded down firmly against the ladder, and the ladder stile, or edge, must be of the rounded type to leave the proper form for the next 'Loun', the term used for the width thatched. The ladder is taken away carefully to leave the hollowed shape to receive the rushes of the next loun in such a way as to make sure that rain will not penetrate as it would do if a poor joint were made. Each handful of rushes is combed, laid firmly, pegged and tied down until the stack is completely covered. The combings go to the next stack for use in peaking.

As regards the round ricks, the loun is of a necessity triangular and the peak often decorated with an imitation sheaf. If the stack or rick was where it could be seen from a road or path, extra care was taken to do a nice job and so issue a silent challenge to other thatchers in the neighbourhood.

So much for the hay and the corn, but what of the animals on the farm? In order of importance the horses must come first, without them it would not have been possible to carry on, they provided the motive power for the whole operation and in addition the mares were used for breeding stock either for sale or replacement. Actually they become very near to being members of the family.

Rarely did you see a farmer and his horse alone, for there was a third member of the group and that was of course the dog. These three out in the fields formed such a complete set, all in harmony, good company, often the farmer with his team—ploughing, harrowing, sowing—and the dog or dogs curled up in the sun or shade, just there if their master should require them and content to be where he was. They formed a sort of entity that has been lost with the advent of the internal combustion engine.

There has been talk about cruelty in the training of animals to make them perform certain tasks. I can assure you that true farmers value their animals too highly to ill-use them. If you lose the trust and regard of these animals it could prove disastrous. What could be more awful than trying to work with a frightened animal?

If the dog is required to collect the sheep or maybe cattle it is commanded, (with the appropriate hand signal giving the direction left or right) to 'Get by' or if quite a distance away 'Get away by', and if in the distance the command is 'Get away off out', and when the dog has gone past and around the animals it is told to 'Bring them on', whereupon the trained dog will carefully and without harassing the animals bring them to you without any further instruction even if there happens to be some unwilling animals present. If told to 'Stand' or 'Stand there' the dog will stand where it receives the order, and a well-trained dog will not move for any reason without being told to do so. This may seem a little hard on the dog if one animal tries to escape, for the nature of the dog is to prevent such an occurrence. But when cutting out one or more animals from a flock it is essential that the selected animals are allowed to part away from the main bunch and when parted the dog is instructed to 'Come in' and so effectively block off any attempt to regain the main body of animals. To 'Lie down' the dog does just that and lies and waits for the next order which may be almost anything (in dog phraseology) depending on what is required, or in which way the animals react to the situation in which they find themselves.

Sometimes the distance is too great for the voice to carry even to the keen hearing of the dog, so the dog was also trained to react to a whistle, either with just the mouth or more often with the aid of two fingers of each hand placed in the mouth and used to produce a sound that a dog could hear a mile or more away.

It follows of course that to be a success the farmer has to be adept as a trainer, otherwise he would be at a very great disadvantage as regards quantity and quality of work to be done. He also has to be an animal psychologist, and I hesitate to use the term for many people who describe themselves thus lack the experience for a complete understanding of the way that man and animal respond to each other. Generations of experience handed down over the years gives this rapport even though the trainer was educationally illiterate.

Often the children had to handle lambs and chickens, work dogs, lead and ride ponies, collect sheep and cattle, all from a very early age and in this way learned how an animal reacts in any particular situation or circumstance. Growing older they understood the feeling and thought of these animals far better than by reading all the text books that have ever been written.

Animals also have a sense of humour! Have you ever had a dog retrieve a ball, offer it to you then whip away just as you go to grab it? Then he runs away a distance, drops the ball and looks at you with his tail doing nineteen to the dozen? Then he picks it up, brings it to you and drops it at your feet with a look that says as plain as speaking: 'That fooled you, eh!'

I must admit that the 'fun' was not always appreciated on the human side. Fanny, the pony, was turned out to grass as soon as there was enough on the fields, and always in the most convenient field so as to be immediately available. This was where Fanny had her fun. You opened the stable door and the field gate into the farmyard, then went into the field to catch her. Just as Fanny reached the gate, she would gallop past it right to the far side of the field where she threw up her head, shook her mane, and neighed a true 'horse laugh', then trotted up through the gate and into the stable. She had had her joke and you had lost ten minutes, but because of the way that it was done, who could grudge Fanny her little joke on account that she made up for it many times over.

A lot has been said and written of late years of animal language and communication both amongst themselves and as to how much can be understood by humans. Certainly a lot has been learned from the scientific study of whales and dolphins, but the fact remains that communication has and does take place between animal and animal, (not necessarily of the same breed) and between man and animal.

Any farmer worth his salt knows the animal sounds and knows what that sound means. Often the sound made by an animal is a greater indication of the condition of that animal than its appearance, at least in the short term. The moment a farmer wakes you could say that his eyes and ears open at the same time. He hears the wind, rain, a blackbird singing, a cow 'bellucking', or lowing, for her calf. The way or tone of the belluck imports information to her calf or the other cattle in the herd. The farmer, from experience, also understands the message. It may be that she wants her calf, to be milked, or is hungry, and the farmer will know whether the message is urgent or the cow is just sounding off to hear her own voice—oh yes, animals do it as well! If it is a call to her calf, the calf replies and says 'I'm hungry', or if not, just answers her call.

Most people think of the stock bull as a fearsome animal, but this is not usually the case, for he is a placid contented creature unless disturbed or interrupted in the course of his normal duties. On the other hand, a cow with a new-born calf is considered to be a lovely docile mother. But beware, if she thinks that her calf is threatened, and this does not take a lot of doing—a small, strange dog or a too curious person—and the beautiful cow turns into a charging bawling demon, with tongue out, eyes wide and staring, enough to frighten a large dog let alone a small one, or a person foolish enough to get too close. A cow in this state would charge an elephant and is far more dangerous than a bull.

The farmer, if in hearing, would know what was happening and get to the scene as soon as possible and, being known by the cow, would be able to calm the situation, hopefully before any permanent damage was done. Peace is at last restored, the cow in licking her calf stimulates it to suckle, and so soothes the nerves of all concerned. Satisfied, the calf lies down close by while the cow returns to the serious business of eating, giving the calf a low burbling sound to reassure it without even stopping grazing. The calf, happy and fed, is either too sleepy or too lazy to respond and just flicks its tail and goes right to sleep and will stay that way until hungry or mother calls it again.

A cry or fright or alarm from the calf—an abrupt blurp sound, very different from the normal call—will bring about a similar animated reaction from the cow. Mother and offspring call to each other and understand each other. There are calls like 'Where are you?' And if the answer is 'Here', both go on grazing contentedly.

The extent of these 'languages' is very much underestimated, but animals ask each other for food, or natural favours, and are accepted or refused as the case may be, whether the request is made vocally or by body language, a much maligned term these days. Likes and dislikes are common, a pecking order is established and maintained, through rivalry at first and afterwards by common consent.

Not only do the animals communicate amongst themselves, but with us as well. Everyone has seen a dog taught to beg, well when an animal likes something it will find a way to ask for it, and so often this asking is unnoticed or misunderstood. There again, if the

Young Farmers Junior Club at Llanbister New School. My brother Jack is sixth from the right, aged 10 I was still too young

animal does not like what is being done to it, it will show its feeling in no uncertain way.

A sad note occurs when a cow or ewe loses her calf or lamb and the mother calls continuously but to no avail. After a while she pauses before calling again. In due course a certain sadness and a sort of hopelessness creeps into her voice and eventually she only makes an occasional call as a last hope. When a cow or ewe loses its young, every attempt is made to find a substitute. In the case of a lamb it is not too difficult, one of a pair is stolen, if possible before the ewe giving birth realises that she has produced two and so does not miss it. This lamb is taken and suckled on the other ewe. Gradually the mother instinct overrides her knowledge that it is not her own lamb and she accepts it as her own.

On two occasions I have been privileged to have seen pairs of 'split' twins appearing to recognize each other a few weeks later. When a pair of twins are split the couples are kept apart for some time to avoid confusing the 'mothers' as to whose is whose. This was done in the two cases, and in due course the two ewes and lambs were put out on the same pasture. In both cases there was no difficulty for the ewes, and no trouble with the lambs suckling, but the two lambs, natural siblings, became mates and stayed that way until the autumn, playing together, grazing and even lying and sleeping together. Once, maybe chance, twice, not in my understanding.

With the loss of the calf the situation is quite different. Cows do not normally have twins so the only way to fill the gap is to buy a calf from a milk farm, where calves are more or less a by-product. You then have to persuade the cow to accept the calf. It takes a bit of patience and a few kicks from the unwilling foster-mother, but patience has its own reward.

In what order farm animals should be placed in terms of intellect and intelligence is rather difficult to decide, for the reason that there is such a difference in the requirements and the way in which their intelligence is used. How much is instinct? How much due to breeding and domestication? Is man more intelligent now than he was a thousand years ago? If so why does or does not this apply to our domesticated animals? Does the fact that these animals no longer have to fend for themselves have any bearing? Or has their association with the human animal brought about any difference or alteration in their mental abilities? Certainly, selective breeding has had a massive effect on the animals' physical characteristics, but has this breeding increased the individual animal's intelligence, or even eliminated the lower or lesser intelligent?

But animals definitely have memories or instincts, for they can find their way home from many miles away even if taken from home in a vehicle. A cow or a horse if returned after years away will go to the stall or stable where it was housed before it went away, though there is no real evidence to suggest it recognizes any of the herd to which it formerly belonged.

The top of my scale for intelligence is the sheep dog. They have the same values as the horse, but to me a little more personal, a little nearer to man in companionship, a little wider in abilities.

One in particular comes to mind: Shep—long haired, rough, noisy, an uncouth individual. That dog would talk to you in howls, play with you, guard anything or anyone connected with you, climb a ladder, walk a pole, swim the river for the asking, catch spiders, flies or even pick flowers. But he would also do the work on the farm, with both sheep and cattle, and would work for spoken commands, whistle, or to hand signs without a sound being made. You frowned and his tail and ears dropped, smiled and up they came.

Pet rabbits were kept that resembled the wild variety, which Shep would chase across the hillside. By chance the pet rabbits got out of their hutch during one night. Imagine our surprise on opening the house door next morning to find the sheep dog lying down guarding the erstwhile strays, a little frightened but otherwise unharmed. This was Shep.

You told him to 'catch it' or 'pick it' and Shep promptly obliged. On the border of a pasture field wild raspberries grew and were picked when in season to sell on Saturday. On going to bring the cows one day Shep was asked to 'pick it' and to our surprise ate it and kept eating. The sequel to this was that Shep was banned from accompanying us when picking raspberries, and instructions were given to keep Shep away from them at our peril.

It could be said that a bark is a bark, but there are as many different barks as there are dogs making them. Barks can register pleasure, pain, likes, dislikes, loves, hates, almost anything. In the hate line there is a range right through a growl to a snarl, all giving a message to master, friend or foe.

Cats are quite different. They learned to come when called for a pan of milk or scraps but apart from that were left to their own devices catching rats or mice. The cats were always handled when kittens to get them accustomed to being caught for any reason when fully grown. This ensured that they were friendly and well behaved, but their home was the farm buildings and they were seldom seen in the house.

Chickens, or more correctly hens, have their place in the scheme of things. Undemanding creatures, they are content to 'scrat', or scratch, for their living where no other creature would even look, and would be given a small feed of grain twice a day to make sure that they kept healthy and strong for laying. It has to be said that hens have a very limited communication system. Amongst themselves they 'talk', but this talk seems nothing but a companionable noise, though in itself it is soothing and has much the same effect as watching goldfish in a tank. If hens are startled, say by a fox, stoat or strange dog, the hens flutter about and make a cackling as if to intimidate the intruder.

A disturbed broody hen gives a clucking sound and is very loth to leave her nest, and anyone putting a hand near is likely to get a sharp jab from her beak. She will continue to use this cluck when chicks are hatched, together with a 'pluck-pluck-pluck' noise to call the chicks if she has found some tit-bits for them. Incidentally the old rooster uses exactly the same tone and tactics to entice the unwary or the willing if he is feeling amorous.

Tiny chicks are a prize for the sparrowhawk, and if there's a chicken in the neighbourhood there's a sparrowhawk. Should the hen or the roost cock spot the hawk they let out a prolonged 'squawk', the hen immediately squats and the chicks take cover under her and hopefully all reach safety before the hawk can get a chick. This taking cover by the chicks is totally instinctive for if you have a brooder, and chicks one day old hear a similar squawk, they will rush back into the brooder as fast as they can go.

Geese are quite different. There is more of a family atmosphere, a little Victorian maybe. The gander is the Victorian father and lets everybody know it! He is very aggressive and actually dangerous, particularly during mating and rearing seasons, and anyone who takes chances would be likely to get a good beating from his wing knuckles, an experience not invited a second time.

With geese there is quite a wide variation of call and tone. When grazing, geese talk just like people working together, even to the occasional raised voice, often for no visible reason as far as humans can see. When a disturbance occurs and one sees or hears something, he or she lets out a loud squawk, taken up by the others, all gazing to see the cause. If none is spotted, grazing is resumed with the normal chatter. If there is reason, the gander struts forth, neck stretched to fullest extent, telling all and sundry who he is and what he is going to do. On approaching the intruder, he puts his head forward, stretches his wings, spreads his tail, whilst the squawk is replaced by loud hissing, all calculated to strike terror to the timid and the not so timid alike. The intruder seen off, the gander does a fair imitation of a victory dance, shuffles wing and tail feathers back to normal and returns to the family, verbally beating his chest like a victorious gorilla. He is received back into the family circle with great acclaim, proudly accepted as becomes a bird of his importance and prowess.

Wild birds also tell their messages. The one that everyone knows of course is the cuckoo, much maligned but always a welcome sound in the countryside for its arrival spells the end of winter and presages better times to come. The blackbird on his perch as high as he can get gives the same message. Peewits wheel overhead, swallows and martins build, swifts scream by in an exhibition of synchronized flight in a model of togetherness that man cannot achieve. All these tell a story that can be read by the countryman. Swallows and swifts flying at ground level to feed, means flies are keeping near to the ground and indicates bad or wet weather. If flying high it tells the opposite for it means air pressure is high and the insects are rising. If a curlew coming in to her

A group of Young Farmers Club members from Breconshire and Radnorshire who attended a course at the University College of Wales at Aberystwyth. I am seated second from right

sleeping ground for the night screams to earth, it presupposes a bad day tomorrow, but if she glides in gracefully, crooning smoothly, then all will be well.

Another indication of the day's weather is that if free range hens are shut in at night and let out in the morning to be fed and it is raining but will clear, the fowls will feed and go back into the fowlhouse and wait for the rain to stop. But if the rain is set for the day, they will stay out in the rain until they have satisfied their hunger, that is unless it is extremely cold.

Again, after the cows are milked in the morning and turned into the field and sense it is likely to rain by about midday, they will lie down and chew their cud until it starts to rain when they will get up and graze. Incidentally, cows busy grazing at 6 a.m. bodes ill for the following day.

The actions of the rabbit foretell how long snow may last. As well as his 'bury', or burrow, the rabbit has his 'squat', a sort of hide or nest in the long grass or undergrowth in a nice dry place where it can sit and digest its feed in comfort. If snow has fallen during the night, the rabbit goes out to find its breakfast. If the snow is going to thaw quickly, it will return to the burrow, but if the snow is likely to last, it will make its way to the squat to sit out the snowfall.

Why this is so, I don't know, but the fact is that this is the cause of many a rabbit getting caught, as the tracks in the snow give the show away.

The hare is a little more devious. It too has a squat, or more correctly a form, to which it returns at or near daybreak, but in a very different manner to the direct approach used by the rabbit. It often passes the form at a distance, then does an about turn and retraces its steps, before jumping to one side three times, landing each time with all four feet together, and on the third jump landing at the entrance to the mouth of the form. But the hare gives no weather indications in its use of the form.

Sheep also give indications of impending bad weather by deserting the high ground and seeking shelter where it is shady. This is not always to the good as far as the sheep are concerned, for where it is shady and out of the wind is where the snow gathers and in heavy snowfall the sheep are buried and have to be dug out, the old faithful and intelligent sheepdog indicating where each sheep is hidden.

*　*　*　*　*

After his family, the rent, food and clothes were the most important things in the farmer's life. Anything saleable was often used to find enough money for the rent—any farm produce that could be sold, any economy that could be devised, in fact anything to help. Often a stock animal had to be sacrificed. Chickens were hatched, reared, fattened, dressed and sold along with eggs, butter and rabbits which had been snared. Rabbits were rarely shot, for cartridges cost $1^{1}/_{2}$d each, and on average a farmer would miss one time in three, making a cost of $2^{1}/_{4}$d per rabbit, against an income of 8d or 9d.

A shopping order for the following week would read something like: 4lbs of white sugar—incidentally this was 'crystal' sugar, 2lbs of brown sugar, 1lb of currants or raisins, $^{1}/_{4}$lb of Typhoo tea, 1lb of candles (twelves, for eighteens were too slender and tended to run down the sides if there was any draughts), $^{1}/_{2}$lb of cheese when there was no cheese being made, 1oz of yeast for baking, and—the only luxury—1oz of twist tobacco for my father.

If there was money over after the order was paid for, it went to pay for clothes or shoes, or paraffin for the lamp in order to work after dark. Candles usually served for lighting, but if there was homework to do it was done on Sunday night with the help of the lamp, which was considered quite a luxury.

Breakfast was variable, the standby at all times was bread and cheese for the adults with bread and jam or bread and butter, and the operative word is 'or'. Bread, butter and jam came later when things got a little better.

Often the Sunday dinner was boiled bacon and then cold boiled bacon was an option for Monday breakfast, not often taken up by the younger ones unless it was nice and lean.

Dinner as often as not was a further helping of yesterday's bacon, with potatoes and possibly swedes mashed either separately or together. If times were good a tablespoonful of cream was mixed with a small quantity of broth from the pot for gravy, which we called 'stump'. It was lovely and creamy, it was good, it was wholesome, and it 'stuck to your ribs' (lasted until the next meal) especially if it was followed by a good helping of Spotted Dick, or fruit dumpling to top off the dinner.

An alternative to boiled bacon was fried, this mostly on a Friday. Why Friday? As the eggs were cleaned for the grocer to collect on Thursday, there were always some which were unsaleable—a few had weak shells, or a double yolk—and therefore became an article of our food, with the number made up to one each for Friday's dinner. Fresh meat from the butcher's was almost unheard of except maybe for Christmas dinner. The only fresh meat was a snared or shot rabbit, roast with fat bacon in the oven, or boiled with vegetables and thickened with flour to make a stew. If a fowl should get hurt by some means that was a luxury.

Such a thing as school dinners were unheard of and the schoolchild's dinner was, without fail, jam sandwiches. I still have a hang up about jam sandwiches. A good chunk of home-made cake followed and that to a certain extent made up for the monotony.

A change occasionally came in the form of beef dripping. When selling chickens or butter, the cooks at the boarding houses or hotels could be persuaded to save the beef dripping and, favour given and favour taken, a large tin of dripping materialised.

Tea for the older members was generally bread and cheese or, for variety, bread and jam.

What excitement there was if we heard that someone was coming to visit. Out came the best china and whilst we had to wait until the visitors had had their tea before we could have any, the ban on butter and jam on the same piece of bread, this time thinly-sliced, was lifted. You could also see the colour of the tea in our cups! Not that we were given the best china cups.

Home from school, it was fried bacon and egg, or ham when ham was on the go, with maybe tart and custard, or fruit and custard.

Supper was quite a variety. The broth from boiling the Sunday joint was filled to capacity with cubed potatoes, swedes, carrots or parsnips, liberally peppered, served hot in basins with as much home-baked bread as was wanted. Another supper was just plain bread and milk, the milk boiled and poured boiling over a basin of cubed bread. When it was plain bread and milk, the milk was fresh and unskimmed, but if all the cream was required, skimmed milk was used and a handful of oatmeal or crushed oats was added to the saucepan with a pinch of salt, and in the same way boiled and poured over the bread in the basins.

Potato soup was another staple. The potatoes were boiled and mashed, new or skimmed milk added, together with prepared lentils or split peas seasoned to taste, and I liked mine peppery! Porridge too of course. Not for breakfast and not with salt, but for supper and with brown sugar and lashings of new milk. Welsh Rarebit was another favourite, when cheese was available—it bore no resemblance to today's recipe, and contained potatoes, streaky and onions.

We never needed to leave the table hungry, for if you didn't have enough it was your own fault, and if you were too fussy to eat what was on the table, too bad, there was no alternative. The food was wholesome and sustaining, a very valuable requirement where long days and heavy work was constant and regular.

Clothing was a major concern. Every means at our disposal was brought into use to economise, whether it was darning, repairing or making over for a smaller member of the family, or remade into something else for the same person.

One important item of clothing suffered greatly from wear—socks. No matter what the job, it involved walking, and walking in hobnailed boots just murdered socks. As children we walked six miles each day to school and back, not to mention the distance that was run in play during the day, also in heavy boots.

Socks were knitted by hand by Granny. When one cares to think about it, it was her way of helping her children and at the same time prolonging her own useful life.

Looking back I remember Grandsir, as we called him, dressed in his Sunday best, or 'Sunday go to meeting clothes'. The coat, for it was more a coat than a jacket, reached to mid or lower thigh and was pleated and split at the back with two cloth covered buttons, with the same sort of buttons to fasten the front. It should have been, and most likely had been, black, but to me it looked some sort of velvety green, and to this day if I see material anywhere near that colour, Grandsir immediately appears in my mind.

This particular coat came to a sad or laughable end, depending on which way you look at it. Grandsir came to visit, and as was usual went with father to 'look around the place'. On this occasion it was just after shearing, and the benches were still on the floor in the barn. It was early June, with the weather probably hot, so Grandsir hung his coat on a nail on a timber in the barn. As it happened a puppy was being reared for a sheep dog and the puppy, the bench, and the coat were the ingredients for disaster. The pup climbed or jumped up on the bench and those green buttons were too good to miss.

My father's best suit was of blue serge. The tie was not always black, but mainly so with a little colour to relieve it, though for funerals, if a man appeared with anything but a black tie he would be considered to be insulting the dead person, and treated in an appropriate manner.

Most of the men of his generation had a pair of 'best' shoes, actually boots, but better quality than the hobnailed variety worn for work. They were always black—I do not think that a pair of brown boots could be purchased at this time.

Women's shoes, as they were called then (ladies were the womenfolk from the Hall), were leather for every day, sturdy and strong to stand the rigours of the land as well as the house, and in many cases had studs in the soles. These studs were flatter in shape and not so heavy as the hobnails but served the same purpose in taking the punishment that would cause leather on its own to wear out very quickly. However, they were hammered into the sole of the shoe in a much more open pattern than that for men's shoes, to reduce the weight to a minimum.

Best shoes were a better quality than the everyday type and were never worn except when on the hard road when going to chapel or to market. The every day shoes were worn if it was wet and until the 'main' road was reached when they were changed and the old shoes hidden in the hedge upside down in case of rain, to be reclaimed on the way home. Should the road be wet, galoshes were pulled on over the shoes to preserve the shine, until the destination was reached.

The housewife's 'best clothes' were worn for all occasions and almost always the same, dark dress or blouse and skirt with a dark coat, with a little white when the occasion allowed.

As always, the first part of a blouse or dress to show signs of wear were the sleeves, so instead of making or buying a new garment, sleeves were made, the sleeves of the dress cut short and hemmed and the 'new' sleeves pinned to the cut off ones. The difficulty was that the coat had to be kept on to hide the deception. However, a pair of black and white sleeves could be interchanged to give the impression of different dresses, and the garment could be worn in summer as short sleeved.

The coat was invariably black, no matter what the style, but always knee length or longer, shorter was deemed to reveal the character of the wearer as well as the knees—a little of the Victorian thinking still extant.

The farmer himself had to have rough and hard wearing clothes, no matter what they looked like. They also had to be serviceable in rain, hail, or snow. One such hard-wearing cloth was described as Derby tweed, a speckled grey cloth, very closely woven to resist the penetration of thistles and thorns. One disadvantage of this sort of material was that it was almost impossible to repair, and I have a sneaking suspicion that attempts to repair it had something to do with the rise of the Farmer Giles image and the jokes associated with him, often as funny to the object of the jokes as anyone else.

An alternative to the Derby tweed outfit was what was called a sleeved waistcoat, very much favoured by men who had to do a lot of hedging on account of its resistance to thorns and the like. The fronts were corduroy, very similar to the usual waistcoat but longer in the body, fastened with six or eight buttons in the usual way of a waist coat. The main difference was in the sleeves and back, which were made with a cloth described as 'Mole-skin', a very closely woven material with a fine smooth texture which provided quite a good resistance to rain.

Shirts were flannel with long sleeves, seldom worn down to the wrists but rolled up to give freedom of movement of the arms, and up out of the way if the job was wet or dirty. No collar of course, who wanted a collar to catch a sheep anyway? But they had a button hole in the centre back for a stud for fixing the collar for Sunday wear. They were always of a non-descript colour with just a stripe— as was said in a joke, so as to know whose shirt it was! Legs were clad in corduroy trousers.

The one article that stamped the housewife as a working woman was the 'Rough Apron'. A hessian sack was cut into two pieces, about eighteen inches wide by twenty-four long, hemmed, and two 'ties' long enough to tie around the back at the waist were stitched on the corners. In this way there was one to wear and one in the wash and this process continued until the apron was almost devoid of colour or eventually worn out. When this final stage was reached the apron became a cloth for washing the stone floors in the house, and if you can think of any use for it after that you ought to be a farmer's wife.

With the children the tactics were rather different. Only good quality shoes were bought for the simple reason that when one member of the family out grew the shoes there was plenty of wear for the next in line. This principle was followed for every day and best shoes, and if possible shoes that were equally suitable for girls or boys in their younger days. As they got older they had to have either girls or boys if they were to avoid being ridiculed, and let it be said that nothing hurts a child more!

Baby clothes were a mystery. They arrived with a 'Let us have them back when you have finished with them', a way of saying that it was not placing the expectant mother under any sort of obligation or sense of patronage, but helping out as they themselves were helped when in similar circumstances. Until about two years of age boys and girls were dressed alike, in petticoats of a cotton type material, knitted pullovers, jackets and of course nappies. The use of petticoats meant that in warm weather no nappies were necessary, and so saved a little work and money. Small as it may be, it counted. Looking at the child it was difficult to know whether it was a girl or boy, apart from the hair style.

Girls had a cut that was jokingly called the 'pudding basin' cut, with a fringe over the forehead and with sides and back to just below the ears and the same length around the back. The boys had two styles, the 'short back and sides' and the 'bob-shorling'—a short fringe over the eyes and all the rest of the head cut really short. This cut had much in its favour—ever tried to make a school boy keep his hair combed up tidy? This was an ever tidy cut, but the real advantage was that it provided no cover for the dreaded head-lice, which were to be found in most schools.

The girls grew up into little pinafore dresses, colourful and easy to make, whilst the boys as often as not had little sailor suits.

The first child was the most expensive as everything was a fresh start, whereas the second had the use of the leftovers from the first, with some additions on account of wear.

The coat for everyday wear was anything that could be called a coat. More often than not the farmer's wet weather coat was a 'Gopsil Brown' sack—a four bushel hessian sack—slung around his neck and fastened with a three inch nail or a piece of fencing wire commonly called a 'bag 'uck'—bag hook.

Given everything, the health of the children in these days was very good indeed, part of the reason being that the village was an entity and infection was less likely than when travel became more general.

All in all they were happy days. Oh yes, we grumbled when shoes pinched or the seat in one's trousers came apart in school—I spent one whole afternoon once with my back to the wall for just that reason, one of the longest schooldays of my life. Times were hard but we had never seen better so we accepted it and now, looking back, I realise that it gave a better value to the rest of our lives.

CHAPTER IV
The Farmer's Wife's Week

Sunday was totally different to any other day of the week. It was a day of rest and was kept as Sunday was meant to be. People were Church or Chapel goers and observed Sunday for that reason if no other, but a day of rest was also necessary after six days of twelve hours or more, mostly engaged in work of a physical nature. All jobs that would otherwise have to be done on Sunday were completed on Friday or Saturday—chopping wood for the fire, carrying water, putting animal feeds and fodder handy.

Sunday started a little later than other days, maybe half an hour or so, but having animals to attend to, a lie-in as such was not possible. Milking the cows and suckling the calves had to be done no matter what the day or what the weather, and the animals fed and watered likewise.

If there was a hired man, he was the 'Waggoner' and was responsible for the horses and their welfare, even on Sundays. In return he had a day off when he wanted one, and because of the goodwill between 'boss and man', the arrangement worked very well.

In the house priority was given to the Sunday dinner, generally the biggest dinner of the week. The big oval cast iron pot was placed over the fire and half filled with water into which was placed a lump of home-produced bacon. It was allowed to boil for a while, then potatoes and other vegetables added in stages so that all were fully cooked at the same time.

This was followed by 'Dumpling', not the tiny indigestible balls favoured in recent recipes, but a real dumpling, a foot or more long and four inches in diameter. About a square foot of dough about a quarter of an inch thick was rolled out, fruit placed on top to cover all but an inch from the sides, sugar added to taste, edges moistened, then rolled up and ends folded in at the same time. It was then rolled in a well-floured clean white cloth, again the ends were closed but all was loosely wrapped to allow for expansion, otherwise it would become a soggy mass. Finally the dumpling was tied up with string, salvaged from the weekly grocery parcel.

Once cooked, it was ceremonially laid on a serving dish, unrolled and sliced, two slices per person, a little more sugar if required and a generous helping of new milk, nectar for the family!

After the meal it was all hands to the washing up and putting things 'by', then it was time for a snooze, the weekly paper or a book until it was time to get tea in time to go to Chapel, unless the weather was too bad. Then it was back home to supper and bed, right to start another week of another month of another year.

As it always has been since the days of the cavemen, so I believe, Monday was, is, and will be, washing day. So Monday morning dawns and sure and certain washing is 'on the menu'. Washing day actually began on Saturday or Sunday with the changes of shirts, socks, dresses, sheets, blankets etc.

Water had to be carried from 'The Spout'. Up on the hill was a spring which was channelled through the rock and a waterfall formed where a bucket could be held to catch the clean water as it fell into a reservoir from which the animals drank. The spout was about 50 or 60 yards from the house, which was as near as it could be brought by means of an open channel. It meant that all clean water had to be carried from there, except for any that came off the house roof and was held in water butts. Some 20 to 30 gallons were required for a washing for a family of seven, and before going to school we did our bit by carrying a couple of buckets of water each to at least fill the fountain on the kitchen fire.

The 'Furnace' was also ready for lighting, wood having been chopped on Saturday. Once both were going full blast, out came the bench from under the back-kitchen table, once the best shoes had been taken off it having been left there after getting home from Chapel the previous day. On it, from right to left, went first the Big Bath, in which went the wash-board, a wooden frame with horizontal ribbing on which the washer-woman rubbed the dirty clothes using plenty of soap and hot water. Next went the Little Bath, used for rinsing after the washing had had the full treatment in the big bath. Next, a final rinse in the Tub, and then they were wrung out ready to go out to the line.

The big bath and washboard

First to be washed were white clothes, sheets and, most important of all, the white Damask table cioths—a house-wife's reputation depended on the whiteness and laundering of her whites. So the routine was whites washed in the big tub, followed by a rinse in the little tub, but then the process differed for the whites from the other washing. It was now transferred to the furnace to be boiled. Here was used the washing powder of that era—Restu or Rinso. While these were boiling the rest of the washing was being done. But to finish with the white clothes—they were now given a rinse— wrung out and put in a vessel with a cube of Reckitt's Blue wrapped in a piece of cloth in the water until the desired strength was obtained. The idea was to give a blue-white finish.

Socks, overalls and badly soiled clothing were subjected to a session on the washboard in the big bath. On completion, the water from the first bath was too dirty for any further use except possibly to water the rhubarb if the weather had been dry for a while. The remaining water, with the exception of the blue water, was used to scrub the stone floors and swill down the cement walkway approach to the door. Sandwiched in the middle of this activity was dinner which had to be made and eaten, and by the time the washing was finished we schoolchildren would be home, hungry as usual, maybe a cut knee to be attended to or buttons to be sewn on. And so to supper and bed, and if we thought we were tired,what must our washer-woman mother be like?

Tuesday was almost a continuation of Monday as the clothes from yesterday had to be ironed and put away. An old blanket was spread on the kitchen table and then covered by a piece of sheet that was in the last stages of survival. First the 'Flat irons' had to be heated by fixing the base of the iron to hooks over the bars of the open fire. This had been prepared in such a way as to have a red hot charcoal base, so that the foot of the iron was free from soot as would be the case with a smoky fire.

When sufficient time had elapsed the iron was taken from the fire with an iron holder comprised of several layers of cloth, and tested for heat. This involved holding the iron up near the face and experience told the user whether it was ready to use or not. If it passed, the base was brushed off with a piece of old dry cloth followed by a quick wipe with a damp one. A quick trial was given on another white piece of cloth and if satisfactory, then and only then was it applied to the all important tablecloths. As the iron cooled, it was used on other things not requiring so much heat, until it had to be exchanged for the other iron. Incidentally a watchful eye was kept on the iron hanging by the fire in case it should get too hot, for surely there was no greater waste of time than having to wait for an iron to cool!

While the ironing was in progress everything was given a good look over to see what needed repair or had reached the end of its current life. Sheets showing signs of wear in the middle were 'Side-to-middled', being cut down their length and, as the process suggests, the outsides were stitched together with a needle—sewing machines were too expensive. If that had already been done, it was cut to make whatever it was good enough for—pillow cases, tea cloths, even hankies, or was maybe put in the First Aid kit to cope with the almost inevitable cut finger or grazed knee, or even put aside for nappies.

Shirts and blouses always seemed to have worn collars and cuffs, socks had holes in heels and toes to be darned, not to mention seats of trousers that needed to be patched and if past repair another cut out and made over from another pair of trousers or jacket that had enough cloth that was serviceable. Patches were a hated necessity and not a fashion as it is today.

When darning became difficult, socks were cut above the heel darning and the stitches picked up and new feet knitted, often with a different colour—but who worried about that anyway!

Any unworn woollen pieces of garments over about six inches square were cut out and put in the 'Rag Bag' to repair similar garments and, failing that, to make quilts for the beds. Woollen cloth was also bought from jumble sales to supplement the Rag Bag so as to get a sufficient quantity to complete a quilt. These bought pieces were often more colourful so as to make a brighter design, for some of these quilts were not only useful they were beautifully made and artistically designed. The cloth was cut more or less to set square or triangular sizes and then sewn by hand to form the required size, before the quilt was stretched on to the quilting frame. This was similar to the modern embroidery frame and measured about seven feet square and was adjusted by a system of pegs and holes. The quilt was now 'lined', generally with nearly worn out woollen blankets, so as to give a complete second layer. (Incidentally these blankets were made from the farmer's own wool by the local woollen mill). The underside of the quilt was the only real expense as a complete piece of cloth was desirable.

During the whole process the frame was supported on four chairs, one at each corner, and the 'seamstress' had to work standing and using the needle up through and down through, one stitch at a time. Finally, the edges were trimmed and taken from the frame and hemmed, and another quilt went into the bedding cupboard.

If there were sufficient sizeable woollen squares left they were used to make a patchwork cushion often filled with washed sheep's wool, or maybe with feathers. What was left was a lot of odd sizes and shapes but still usable. This woollen cloth was cut into three inch strips roughly one inch wide. A hessian sack with a close weave was found, washed, cut and hemmed to the required size, depending really on the amount of rags available and the closeness of the 'pile' wanted. A rug was then worked from the back. A hole was made with a pointed peg, then a strip of woollen cloth was pushed through the sack with a peg to nearly half way, then another hole was made half an inch away from the first and the remainder of the rag pushed through it. If coloured patterns were desired it was drawn on the back of the hessian and worked to accordingly. Often two people would work on the rug at the same time while sitting by the fire at night. These rugs were placed by the side of the beds, but if the weather was very cold, they were taken off the floor and put on the foot of the bed to warm cold feet.

Wednesday was somewhat different from the other days of the week for it had no really fixed jobs. All depended on what was urgent or seasonal, or even whether the day was wet or fine, warm or cold.

Wednesday was mending day, jam

Mrs. Beeton's and pot

making day, gardening day, fruit picking, egg cleaning, (the grocer called at the neighbouring farm on Thursday to collect the eggs and deliver the week's grocery order).

Almost any fruit or vegetable was made into jam, chutney or pickled to provide for the whole of the following year. The ingredients were more or less the same as those used today, but the conditions and equipment were very different. Fruit picking itself could be an effort—plums grow on tall trees and wimberries on the top of the hill, for example. Then the right fire must be arranged so that the jam will not be burned or boil over, next the fruit weighed and the right amount of sugar (ordered the week before last and delivered last week) and water added to the 'jam pot'. If you had called it a preserving pan no-one would have known what you were talking about!

When ready the jam was 'laded' into 2lb jars and filled to within a quarter of an inch of the top. Already prepared would be a saucepan of either fat or wax, heated to form a liquid, and this was poured on to the jam so sealing the jar. The fat would have been rendered down from any edible fat and kept for this purpose, whilst wax came from the bees after taking the honey off in the autumn. Jam covered in this way would keep for as much as two years, and the fat or wax could be melted down and re-used for next year's jam.

Fruit bottling was slightly different. Fruit was washed and put in jars, any jar would do providing it had a smooth neck with a rim to hold a tie string. Big, small, tall, short, fat or slim, if it had a rim, some fruit was put in. These jars were covered with a membrane of pig's bladder—when the pigs were killed for bacon earlier in the year, the bladders were washed and blown up, in much the same way as a balloon, and hung up to dry. The bladder was then cut to size so as to cover as many jars as possible and during fruit bottling was placed in warm water to make it flexible for use. The jars were filled with fruit and water, then the membrane was tied down, and here a little expertise was required, for if not tied firmly the whole operation would be a failure. The jars would then be placed in the oval boiler pot, being kept away from the bottom, sides and each other with clean hay. This was then placed over the fire and slowly brought just to the boil, then allowed to slowly cool. This process created a vacuum in any space left under the bladder.

Thursday was different to other days of the week for the job to be done was actually started on the Thursday of the previous week. Thursday was Baking Day. First, the 'oven wood' was taken out of the oven, and this was where today's baking had started last week, for the wood had been chopped and put in the still hot oven to dry out once the bread had been taken out. This oven resembled a low, wide cave, turtle-shaped with a slightly domed roof, the upright walls maybe six bricks high.

The dry wood was used to light the fire, as little paper was used as possible for it was a scarce commodity. Wood or gorse were used to keep the fire in, never coal. About two hours was needed to get a good baking heat. It could be done much quicker, but would then not maintain sufficient heat or provide an even heat for the length of time required, whilst too much heat meant bread burned on the outside and didn't bake in the middle.

Out comes the bench, the same bench that was used for washing on washing day, and also a galvanised bath—but this one was shining clean. Into it went the required amount of flour in which two hollows were made, and one was filled with water or skimmed milk, possibly buttermilk. If there were plenty of potatoes for the year an amount of cooked and mashed potatoes were put in as it was a means of saving flour, though the resultant bread was not so good.

The yeast was now added, prepared earlier. The weekly grocery order, which was delivered to the neighbour, included one ounce of yeast, for fresh yeast was then easily obtainable as most people baked their own bread. The yeast was crumbled into a basin with a teaspoonful of brown sugar and a small amount of water, and put to stand in a warm place—the resulting fermentation was said to 'prove' the yeast.

If the yeast did not prove, thankfully very rare indeed, panic ensued. As not all people baked on the same day, there was generally one of the neighbours who would have some yeast available, to be replaced before they wanted it. Everything being in order, the yeast mixture was diluted with warm water and added to the second hollow.

Both liquids were then worked into the flour, very carefully and separately to begin with and later merged together, gradually working the whole of the flour into one large lump of dough. Badly mixed flour resulted in dry areas of flour remaining which formed 'lazy ha'pennies' in the loaves. The bath of dough was then taken and placed in a warm spot near the fire, but not in the direct heat as that would kill the yeast, then covered with a piece of muslin or butter cloth and part of a linen sheet that had 'done its time'.

After about an hour the dough would have risen to fill the bath and it was taken down from its warm place on the hob and kneaded. The bath was replaced on the bench, the cloths taken away and the hands of the housewife were floured and her closed fists were driven down through the dough right to the bottom of the mix, making little blurps and squeaking noises as the yeast bubbles burst. This kneading has the effect of making these bubbles smaller and so giving a finer texture to the finished loaf.

The dough was replaced in the warm to rise again before going through the same process, at the end of which it was formed into loaves ready for baking, and either placed in tins or shaped as round lumps to be baked on the floor of the oven. The dough was then left for a short time to rise once more before being put in the oven.

During all this time the fire was kept going and the art was to get the dough and the oven ready at the same time. When the fire was first started in the oven, the oven's ceiling, walls and floor appeared very dark, almost black in colour, but as the heating progressed, this changed. Starting with the ceiling directly above the fire the colour became much lighter and this change progressed outward and downward.

About the same time as the second kneading took place, stoking was discontinued and the pile of wood allowed to burn down to red hot cinders which were subsequently spread around the base. This was timed to coincide with the last rise of the dough and made certain that an even heat was achieved over the whole base of the oven. When that was the case, the oven was raked clear of cinders and its floor cleaned off with a cloth wrapped around a stick and dipped in water until no dust or ashes remained.

The bread was then put in with the aid of an old spade or something of a similar nature, followed by the cakes which were made whilst the dough was rising. Unlike the bread, the cakes were always put in tins because of the fat that they contained. Then in went the tarts, pies or lardy-jacks, and last of all, to one side, went a piece of ham. I'm sure I can smell and taste that ham to this day!

The oven door was closed and the cinders piled up against it to keep the heat in on the 'mouth' of the oven. After about twenty minutes the cinders were carefully taken from the door, the door ever so gently opened and the tarts literally whisked from the oven and the door gently closed and sealed again.

A little while later the operation was repeated to take out the cakes and the roast ham. After a total of two hours the bread was taken out, the ones in tins turned out and stood upside down on the scrubbed table top, as were the loaves baked on the floor. If you were not hungry before, you were by then.

Baking done, the week's eggs had to be cleaned, if not done on Wednesday, and taken to the neighbouring farm, the nearest place that a motor vehicle could reach—delivery and collection by horse and trap was ruled out because of the time taken. Apart from the eggs, a few rabbits might also be taken in baskets, or if too many, then either on horseback or in the trap.

Friday was 'churning' day. For all of the previous seven days the cows had been milked morning and evening and the cream separated from the milk and stored in cool conditions in the dairy to allow it to mature naturally—really fresh cream is not the best for making butter.

The cream used to be separated in the 'Leads'. Imagine the frame of a table, say three feet by four, which had a sheet of lead hollowed in the centre to a depth of about nine inches in place of the top. This hollow was capable of containing three or four gallons of milk. At the lowest point in the hollow was a drain hole, closed by a plug on a rod that rose above the level of the milk which was poured onto the lead after milking. Two leads were needed, one for each milking, and the milk was left to stand till the following morning or evening. As the milk cooled the cream, being lighter, rose to the surface and thickened, allowing a bucket to be placed under the lead and the plug loosened so that the milk could be drained off, leaving the cream behind.

The farm in Winter

At some point doubts were raised about the use of lead for the preparation of foodstuffs or in pipes to carry water due to the recognition of lead poisoning. So another method was adopted. The milk was poured into large tin pans, three feet in diameter and about six inches deep, and allowed to cool in the same way. But instead of draining the milk, the cream was skimmed from the surface with a 'skimmer' or even with a saucer.

During the twenties a company marketed a cream separator that was much more efficient and also meant there was no pans of milk lying about all the time. This separator worked on the principle of a centrifuge that caused the cream to rise to a higher level than the milk, at which point it was channelled into a separate receptacle. Another of its advantages was that there was no limit to the amount of milk that could be processed at any particular time as there was with the old method of leads and pans.

Once separated, the week's cream was poured into a cool churn. If the churn was too warm it would cause the cream to turn into butter too quickly making butter of a poor quality. In Summer maybe some cold water, direct from the well, was used to cool it, and vice versa in Winter some boiled water was used to warm it. In the lid of the churn there was a small window for the operator to see and judge the condition of the contents. The lid also had a pressure release valve, as for a little while during churning gas was released and the valve was pressed to relieve the extra pressure. But this was only for a short period and churning soon become a steady rhythm.

The actual time taken to cause the change to butter varied depending on the temperature of the contents and the richness of the cream, itself dependent on the time of year and whether it came from cows newly calved, as the quality drops with time. In Winter the quality was likely to be poorest unless a lot of concentrates were being fed to the cows—as likely as snow in Summer! Usually the change occurred after about half an hour, the first indication being a toughening up of the contents. Sometimes it became semi-solid and adhered to the churn, 'it went to sleep' as the expression had it. By jerking the churn backwards and forward it was possible to get movement and the immediate result was the change to butter and buttermilk, true buttermilk, unlike some of the so-called buttermilk used in adverts to sell ersatz butter products. When this separation took place the butter was almost like small shot.

A plug was then partially taken out of the lower part of the churn and the buttermilk drained off. The plug and lid replaced, clean cold water was put in its place and the churn turned slowly to wash off any remaining buttermilk. This was repeated twice more and then the butter was gathered into one lump and put in the 'Trind' also called the 'Mitt' or the 'Butter mitt', with the 'Hands' or the butter pats. The trind was a wooden vessel akin to one end of a barrel, two feet across and nine or ten inches deep, made of oak and banded just like a barrel. The hands or butter pats were similar to table tennis bats, but with a rectangular end as opposed to the round of the bat. They were made of boxwood, in all about a foot in length, smooth on one side and grooved on the other to facilitate handling the butter while working it.

Salt was sprinkled over the butter in the trind and worked in with the hands, both human and wooden. The trind was then flooded with water and the butter, if it was to be used or sold as fresh, was washed to get as much salt out of it as possible—this method apparently leaving the right amount of salt in to make the butter taste good. If the butter was to be stored for winter use, extra salt was added but not washed out. It was then stored in a sterilised 'Stein' (pronounced steen), a salt glazed vessel, and covered with a layer of salt.

The fresh was made up into pounds and half pounds, in much the same shape as butter currently sold in the shops, except that it was usually narrower and thicker. Each housewife made her own design on her butter, forming indentations using the pats, which served to identify the butter to prospective customers. A certain amount of butter was kept for home use, but this was used sparingly so as not to deplete sales.

The churning done, and with the butter destined for market tomorrow ready on a large white dish, it was time for the next tasks. Depending on the time of year there would be chickens to kill and dress or truss, peas to pick and weigh up, (paper bags for this had been saved), wild raspberries to pick or wimberries gathered off the hill.

Saturday was totally different to the other days for it was market day, a clear divergence from the usual and in fact the culmination of the week in as much that it was the money-making day. The pony was harnessed to the trap, a two wheeled light vehicle, sprung and with a seat across the width capable of seating three grown-ups. In front of the seat was sufficient space for the rest of the family on the floor, with cushions to give a little comfort, but who worried about comfort for we were headed for Town, and that was sufficient. Dad held the reins, Mum nursed the baby, Mettle the pony ate up the miles and we kids were in a world of wonder, our world was heaven.

Once when we went on this idyllic journey the road was being repaired and a steamroller started up as we passed. As the engine went 'woof, woof, woof,' Mettle took off at full gallop. The road under us went at a terrific rate and her hooves were banging on the surface. I think that Mother was too terrified to do or say anything and Dad had as much as he could do to keep Mettle on the road. After about three miles Mettle quietened and she slowed down. We all got out of the trap and I well remember Dad leading her to us to stroke and talk to. I'm certain that there were tears in her eyes, and if ever there was an apology made it was made there.

Years later Mettle had to be put down due to a bowel stoppage. I remember when she was ill finding what we thought was a nice bit of grass and taking it to her. She took it from us and made a pretence of chewing it before dropping it because she couldn't swallow it, and I write with tears in my eyes at the memory.

The journey to town had to be undertaken in winter too, but there was a water-proof cover to get under and rugs of odd sizes and shapes in which to wrap up and keep warm.

Llandrindod was then a Spa of high repute which attracted a clientele of importance who not only enjoyed the Waters, but also the gastronomic delicacies of the fresh supplies from the local farming community, to the advantage of both.

The produce was unloaded near the town centre and guarded by one of the family while the pony and trap were taken to The Llannerch pub for parking and stabling. Then one stood with part of the produce while two loaded arm baskets were taken from door to door, selling the goods and taking orders for the following Saturday, returning to base (under a veranda or awning if the day was wet) to restock the baskets.

The eggs clean, nestled in folds of paper, the butter spaced like soldiers on greaseproof paper on a flat bottomed basket, each pat with mother's mark and a band of greaseproof around the middle, like the band on a cigar, so as to avoid touching it during handling.

Peas and beans had been weighed up in packs of one, two and three pounds so making any total weight required. Potatoes and swedes were not taken 'on spec', but orders were taken for the following Saturday.

To us small ones it was a long, long day and we were as glad to start for home as we had been to start from there. Soon the effects of the day and the rhythm of Mettle's hooves on the road told and we slipped away to be awakened when we got home, a little grumpy maybe, but hungry and ready to go to bed without dissent.

Then there was the eighth day. It may sound somewhat strange to talk about eight days in the week, but during this day all that has not been reckoned on has to be done regardless of time and place—the unexpected, good or bad, one-offs or many, accidents, visitors, sick children or animals, or harvest help at a moment's notice.

Farm machinery could be dangerous, with fast moving cogs and spindles, whilst much work involved sharp blades whether in machines or used manually, and that increased the danger of cuts or abrasions. Anyone who has to use or train animals is always at risk, particularly of back injury, bruising and even broken bones. Working on steep slopes on hillsides in wet or winter weather posed quite a risk from slipping. Kids fall and cut their knees or elbows, fall out of trees, turn over with the sledge, fall off the pony, get tummy ache—you name it they do it! The remedy is the nurse and housewife, with her healing hand, a soothing voice and a salve for everything. A kiss will do more to heal a little one than all the remedies in the chemist's shop.

The chemist was six or seven miles away in any event, and the doctor four, so a few remedies were kept in the cupboard—Carron oil for burns and scalds; an ointment called Zam-Buc for bruises that was green and smelled of oil of Wintergreen; Germoline—like

95

Zam-Buc in a small round tin which was hard to open—a nice pink, but not so aromatic; Eucalyptus oil to put on handkerchiefs to clear the nose. Camphorated oil was another item in the medicine chest.

There were always old cures of course—goose oil for chest complaints; black currant tea, an infusion of black currant jam, drank as hot as possible, or better still elderberry or elderflower wine as a cure for colds, the wine version being reserved for adults; tea made from broome was a tonic—almost every farm then had its broome, but it now seems to have found a new home on the sides of the motorways.

But the cure-all was pure turpentine: for cuts, bruises, chilblains, even sore heels. It was a wonderful remedy. Whether it was our faith in it or not I am not certain, but it seemed to work and was cheap. It also smelled nice.

Then there were the children to bring up. The painting, papering and furnishing were also part of the housewife's responsibilities as were the poultry and that included the turkeys and geese for the Xmas market. All in all the eighth day was the busiest of the week, and its work varied with the seasons and the weather.

The story is told that someone not knowledgeable of farming stayed the night and asked the farmer, 'What are you going to do tomorrow?'

'All being well', said the farmer, 'I am going to cut the grass on the Top Meadow to make hay of it.'

Next morning the visitor asked the equivalent question, and got the reply, 'Get the hay in off the Bottom Meadow if I can.'

'Last night you said that you were going to cut the Top Meadow. You know you farmers are as changeable as the wind.'

'Exactly,' said the farmer, 'the wind has changed and it looks as if it may rain before tomorrow.'

At this time such a thing as a fridge on a farm was less likely than flying pigs and so all things had either to be dealt with as and when they were in season or they were lost, and that was a loss for a whole year. After all, there were no stores with all manner of imported fruits and vegetables to fill the gaps.

Every effort was made to get some fruit and vegetables to mature early and others later, and this was also true of poultry and animals. The earlier hens could be 'put to sit', encouraging them to sit on eggs to hatch them, the sooner chickens would be ready for market. A broody hen soon after New Year was a gift not to be ignored, and meant an early brood of chicks.

Some of the older breeds tended to go broody quite often, as a matter of fact, too often, for a broody hen does not lay for something like six weeks. It meant that after a sufficient number of hens have been put to sit, any further broody hens were confined in a manner which did not allow them to follow their natural instincts so as to encourage them to return to laying earlier than if left to themselves.

Day old chicks were a thing of the future, as were brooders, so the natural process had to be used. The usual method was to have a few of the older breeds for their broody tendency and a larger number of the so-called laying strains which rarely went broody. This arrangement not only gave a maximum amount of egg production, but was also a good means of providing replacement laying stock.

Chicks hatched early in the season meant early matured birds for sale in the town, and pullet chicks mature enough to come into lay before Christmas meant eggs at a time when eggs were at their best price.

Turkeys and geese were well fed after Christmas, but not over fed as a fat bird is not a good layer, is not the best for sitting, and is apt to be lazy. This laziness also applies to the male of the species.

A good goose should start laying by St. Valentine's Day and lay on alternate days until there are twelve to fifteen eggs. Two geese were kept, with a gander, and put to sit at the same time if this could be done, and hopefully eggs would hatch in twenty-eight to thirty days. Both hatches of goslings, 'Gulls', or 'Gullies' locally, were put with one goose whilst the second goose was put with the gander somewhere out of sight and earshot of the goslings so that, hopefully, they would mate again and a second hatch materialise. This ploy was also practiced with turkeys, but selective breeding and changed management has now made this unnecessary.

Ducks do not make good sitters or mothers, so a few broody hens were put to sit on duck eggs. Imagine the consternation of the foster mother when her brood took to the water and paddled away quite happily. Still, she remained loyal to her brood, often getting into the water until her feathers touched it, clucking her disapproval and annoyance to no avail, until the ducklings had their fun and decided to do what mum said, but even then leading the way instead of letting mother do what mothers should do. They grew so quickly that 'mother' was soon left hopelessly stranded and eventually she gave up and let her wayward brood go their own way.

Lambing was also a busy time for the housewife. Any lamb that was weakly for reasons of temperature or hunger ended up in the house, given a drop of brandy (denied to the farm personnel except in extreme circumstances) in a little warm milk, possibly ten minutes immersion in blood-heat water, dried with a towel and placed in front of the fire until sufficiently revived. The lamb was then taken back to its mother and suckled, that is given the teat of its mother whilst the base of its tail was tickled. This for some reason stimulates the lamb to suck and so get some of its mother's milk, and especially the colostrum produced in the first few days, which is so necessary to its survival. All this was the job of the housewife and gave the farmer time to look after the other sheep and lambs.

The success of the farming year largely depended on the lambing, a good one—success; a poor one—a struggle. There's no way one can reasonably describe the feeling of either—the elation or the despondency. If the latter, there was no alternative but to carry on and hope for better next year and that the landlord would understand.

With April came rhubarb which, in Biblical language, was the first fruits. A load of horse manure was spread on the rhubarb bed which, providing heat in its decomposition, persuaded the rhubarb to grow earlier than it would otherwise. A further incentive was provided by turning any old bucket or galvanised bath upside-down over it. At a time when there was little or nothing else, it would make jam, dumplings, a sweet with custard and if need be a first class wine for Xmas.

May is one of the finest months of the farming year, full of promise and optimism. The garden has been dug by the menfolk and a liberal application of farmyard manure applied and now it was the turn of the housewife to plant. Usually a few rows of early potatoes would have been planted when the digging was done, and now in went carrots, parsnips, cabbages and leeks. Shallots were put in earlier if conditions were favourable.

By the time June comes a few of the early hatched cockerel chicks will have matured sufficiently to be ready for market, and they produce the first return for the housewife for the year. This brings with it a sense of achievement which is worth more than the actual cash benefit, however important that may be.

Life becomes especially hectic from June onwards. The cows are often flush with milk on the summer grass, and more milk means more cream which in turn means more butter.

Any surplus was made into cheese. The milk was put in a large container with maybe all of the cream, or perhaps half of the cream taken off (to take all of the cream away resulted in a very tough, leathery cheese) and at blood heat rennet was added, stirred well and left to work. By next day the whole had become a little like yoghurt and was 'cut', or stirred in such a way as to cause a breaking up of the structure to produce curds and whey. The whey was drained off and fed to the pigs.

The curd was then lightly salted and gathered into a muslin cloth, the whole placed in a suitably sized cheese vat and put under pressure to squeeze out the last of the whey. Often as not these presses consisted of some weird and wonderful contraption of levers and weights, generally stones or pieces of cast iron from some defunct machinery. After sufficient time or pressure had been applied the cheese was taken out of the vat and cloth and placed somewhere to dry. When fully dry it was stored in the dairy to mature.

All this time the garden was kept up to date—weeding, hoeing, sticking peas and runner beans, the menfolk were generally persuaded to 'bring a few bean sticks back with you'.

Then the gooseberries were ready for making jam or bottling for winter use. For these purposes they were not allowed to fully ripen, otherwise the skins became tough and often bitter to the taste. The better quality fruit was bottled, and here a little pride and rivalry occurred so as to be able to put on a decent show for 'visitors'. Bottled fruit should show no sign of breaking up, in the case of plums the skin should be unbroken, and in general the juice bright and unclouded.

One sort of fruit failed, another had a bumper crop, some came earlier than usual, some later and at the same time the harvesting has to be attended to. If necessary everything else went by the board, the house had to be left and the wife would take the place of an extra man, to wield a pikel or a rake, to drive a horse, to load the hay or corn. In the harvest field there was no His or Hers, Yours or Mine, Young or Old, it was all Ours.

Summer gives way to Autumn, the final gathering of fruit and vegetables, and the potatoes in particular. The menfolk dug the potatoes and the wife and children that were old and strong enough picked them up. All were aware that potatoes were a major contribution to dinners for the next nine months.

The pigs have been roaming around the land made accessible to them and gathered their own food to a large extent—roots, nuts, acorns and of course grass, whilst also being given a little corn meal and all the surplus skimmed milk. By this time they have become sizeable animals. Thoughts turn to salting the bacon and salt was ordered from the grocer and delivered with the weekly order, arriving in the form of solid bars weighing about 20lbs.

Once the pig had been butchered and cut into hams and flitches (the shoulder and flank in one piece), the housewife took over, covering the salting stone with a thin layer of salt crushed from the bars. On this she laid the flitch rind down and covered it with another thin layer of salt. Where the bone showed at the shoulder a mixture of saltpetre and black pepper was applied in addition to salt. The second flitch was then laid on top of the first, and being the opposite shape fitted nicely, and received the same treatment. Finally the hams were notched in and covered as before.

Other parts, the small meats, were not stored for long as they wouldn't keep. Liver, heart and kidneys were cooked and eaten quickly, often being shared with the neighbours who would reciprocate when they killed their pig. The spare rib (the rib cage), and the chines or chimes—the spine, were either not salted at all if designated for immediate use, or only lightly so, for they would be used presently—storing meat where bones protruded was always the most difficult.

Next came the lard. Whilst the carcase was being butchered, all surplus fat was cut away and put in a pot, (the only 'pan' was the frying pan, everything else was boiled, stewed or rendered down in a pot!) and placed over a low fire. Great care was necessary, for too much heat would cause the fat to burn and stick to the bottom of the pot, and if the fat should boil over it could cause a house fire. As the fat melted it was laded off into Steins for storing and this continued until what was left was the 'scratchings'—true scratchings and not some synthetic concoction sold under that heading.

The housewife was also responsible for feeding, dressing and preparing the geese, one of her prime sources of income.

Her year culminated with the Christmas dinner. A goose or turkey had been retained and was destined for her own family, served on her own table, cooked by herself with vegetables she had grown and wine she had made. It was followed by Christmas pudding that she had made last October, served with a good portion of fresh cream.

So now may we wish the housewife a Very Happy Christmas, this year, next year and for all time.

CHAPTER V
People

Until the railway came in the middle of the 19th Century, there was no contact with the outside world except by carriage, on horse-back or on foot. This all changed with the internal combustion engine. People started to get about and saw for themselves how other people fared in comparison, but even then things were slow to change, so that the 'catching up' process took a long time.

The roads in this part of the world form no set pattern except that they follow the valleys and the rivers that flow through them, or cross the ridges to other valleys in a manner that appears at first sight to be haphazard.

The 'main' road ran almost due north-south, following the river Ithon as nearly as was practical and by doing so maintained a more or less constant gradient, a prime consideration in the day of the horse. Generally the towns and villages sat astride the road in much the same way as a string of beads, but at no fixed distances, the towns being the bigger beads and the villages the smaller. Our village was different. It lay off the main road up the steep 'pitch' of Nant-y-Claf. Another oddity was that all the house names in the village were English, whilst those of the farms were Welsh.

The main road was the only one with a tarmac surface, all the others were lined with broken stone from the nearest quarry, often hauled by the local farmers who hired their horse and cart and themselves at so much per day or per load. The stone was then broken down into pieces about one inch in diameter, maybe a little bigger, placed on the road surface and if luck was their way the steamroller rolled it in. But more often than not it was padded down by the passage of horses and carts. Surprisingly, these broken

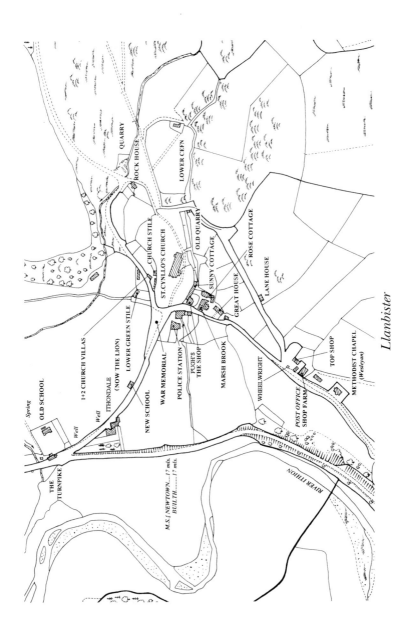

Llanbister

stone roads became reasonably smooth and would stay that way, hard frosts often doing more damage in one night than a year's travelling.

In 1865 the LNWR (The London and North Western Railway Company, later to become the LMS or London, Midland and Scottish Railway) opened the Central Wales Railway with a station near Penybont at Crossgates. Feed-stuffs were now available for collection from the station. However, there was one snag—a full load could be got as far as Nant-y-Claf but extra horses were required to haul the loads up the steep hill. This wasn't a problem for the local farmers, but it was very difficult for people who farmed miles away to have the extra horses available. So, soon after the arrival of the railway, the farmers got together and cut a way through the bank wide enough for a roadway. The result of this 'bypass' was that there was only one house left on the main road, the old Turnpike, sadly no longer there.

No longer used to collect tolls, this was the home of William Price and his sister, Mary. Their mother was 'the Huckstress', who had a donkey and cart which she used to collect farm produce from miles around to take to the Thursday market in Knighton. I don't recall any mention of a husband and I assume that she was a widow and that this was her way of supporting her family. Neither William nor Mary had children of their own, as far as I know, but seemed to keep a second home for nieces. Known as Bill, William had a shed further up and on the opposite side of the road, but didn't seem to have any regular occupation. He was apparently a landowner, though I have a distinct memory of him wearing a postman's coat, but whether he was a postman I am not certain. However, we thought a lot of him as he would occasionally have a homemade piece of toffee for us small ones, much to our gratification and the annoyance of the elder ones. During school dinnertime we quite often dawdled somewhere near 'Bill Price's', always hopeful! He knew why.

I can still see Mary Price standing in the doorway, dressed as a 'Granny' was expected to dress and watching us going through the gate into the schoolyard at the back of the Turnpike. I always had the feeling that if something had been wrong in any way she would have seen to it.

The village roads take the shape of an 'h', with the stem rising first gently then steeply uphill. This road eventually leads over the hills to outlying districts. On entering the stem of the 'h' the old

Mrs. Price, the Huckstress

school, at the back of the Turnpike, comes into sight, separated from the road by the playground, a site now occupied by the Vicarage, but which was then in effect a sloping piece of field. At this time the Vicarage was at least a mile away, and prior to that, according to an old map, was situated in the churchyard itself.

Fifty yards further on was the schoolmaster's house, at one time the Red Lion pub, as lettering on the end wall indicated, and which it is now once more. Then called Ithondale, it was occupied by the schoolmaster and his wife. Mr. and Mrs. Bennett were opposites. He was tall, slender, bald, and severe, a headmaster in every respect, a disciplinarian from head to toe and a perfectionist to boot. A look through his pince-nez called for immediate silence, and a pointed finger made certain that no further misdemeanours occurred for that day at least. But we all respected him and as far as I was concerned he was my idol. Although I had mixed feelings of awe and esteem, he gave me the unrealised ambition of being a schoolmaster.

Mrs. Bennett was short, motherly, and had no children of her own so maybe we filled a gap in her private life. She would bandage a knee, comb your hair (if she thought it wanted doing), or dry your socks.

General view over Llanbister, looking west

As well as the schoolmaster and his wife a couple of spinsters lived there, to our delectation, delight and decadence as Leonard Sachs of the Good Old Days would say. These sisters kept a pair of goats which I have to admit we teased, quite safely too as we could run faster than the Misses Lewis, and also due to the fact that the goats were tethered.

Further on was the New School, a marvellous thing to us, so different, so big and imposing, on level ground, iron railings round the playgrounds, and yes, the girls and boys were separate! Gosh we were Posh! Only the County School in Llandrindod Wells had similar in the county.

The village or at least part of it is now in sight, a hundred yards on up the increasing gradient, and on the left where the junction split off sits the War Memorial, on a levelled grassy patch. This was where any school quarrels demanding physical action were settled with many a black eye or bloody nose, and more than one lesson learned that wasn't taught in the school.

Then, on the left, came Lower Green Stile, better known as 'Tom Mills", or to use the local pronunciation 'Tum' Mills". The house was a tiny two up and two down in which Tom, the shoe-maker or cobbler, would make or mend shoes, horse harnesses, school satchels (school bags to us)—in fact if it could be made of leather Tom made or 'ment' (mended) it. I remember shoelaces cost 1d per pair; he cut them himself from a sheet of leather, short ones for us, long ones for grown ups. If a lace was broken when in school and unusable, Tom cut you one, 'Bring a ha'penny tomorrow'.

He was a pleasant homely chap, a 1914-18 soldier who had lost a leg, but who had engineered a replacement that he worked from a harness over his shoulder so as to lift and and swing his leg forward. One of the downstairs rooms was his 'shop' and often on a cold school day we would go up to Tom Mills' and sit by his small fire to eat our sandwiches, while he thumped away at his last, his shoe-shaped model over which he could fit the shoe on which he was working, and talked to us through a mouthful of 'sprigs', small nails. How I envied him: tip, bump, bump, and the sprig was driven home, and he never, ever hit his thumb. He didn't ever mention the war and I am sure that the omission was intentional. Tom didn't live here, but lodged with a Mrs. Reese in a house in Frog Street.

Before Lower Green Stile was occupied by Tom Mills, a tradesman known as Welsh John had carried on business from there. Welsh John was a carpenter, cabinet maker and undertaker. The story is told that in Winter John would say, 'Tis no' fit no man work today. Too cold, too cold', and on a hot day in Summer 'Tis no' fit no man work today. Too hot, too hot.' But the story most often related is when two coffins were ordered, one for a short person and one for a tall one. A relative of the tall one called and saw the coffin for the other and remarked that the coffin was too short, to which Welsh John is reputed to have replied: 'Wass alright. Wass cut feet off!' Suffice it to say that a satisfactory fit was achieved.

A little higher up the road was the dressmaker, Mrs. Barnett, a widow with two children who lived at Church Villa. She was not seen a lot, but as a seamstress was an asset to the area. She made clothes for children, weddings, funerals, general requirements, in fact whatever was wanted, and at a moment's notice. Her house and small cottage garden were almost hidden by trees and a garden hedge, and one half was occupied by a Mr. and Mrs. Jones and their two children.

Recessed into the churchyard were Upper and Lower Church Stile. The last known occupier of one of these was a man named

St. Cynllo's, Llanbister

John Brown, who was a true shoemaker, as opposed to the cobbler. It was often the case that a man paid for the shoes that he already worn past repair when he put in an order for a new pair. The story goes that, as John Brown came close to retiring age (in those days when too old to do one's work), when a customer called to order a new pair John would say, 'You haven't paid for last year's yet.'

'Oh, that's aright, John,' was the reply, 'I was going to do that now.'

'And,' said John Brown, 'thee'll pay for the next 'afore I'll make 'em too!'

Anyone looking at the church itself will immediately see a difference. The Belfry is at the opposite end of the church to the usual. The story goes that when the church was in the building, the tower foundations gave way. So a new start was made, and strangely enough the same thing happened again. After what I suppose was due deliberation the conclusion was reached that the 'Powers that Be' were displeased and that to put things right the tower should be built at the other end of the church, the theory being that if no

107

fault occurred there then the 'Powers' would be happy. As can be seen the tower stood and everyone was content.

There are steps up to the church door, and on opening the door one is surprised to find several stone steps leading up to the level of the nave within and which contains fragments of murals of considerable age.

Previous to the restoration, so the story goes, the roof and walls did not meet everywhere and as well as the bats, a few crows made their home on the top of the thick walls. Those of the congregation who were forced to sit against the walls during services could have a very uncomfortable service indeed, and the idea that all good things came from above was somewhat doubtful.

Restoration work was carried out in 1908. Money was raised locally, with contributers signing a book, the names later being embroidered on a cloth. Many local names are included, some of them of my own family including that of my father. But some of these signatures are 'mirror' images, indicating that some of the embroiderers could not read and so transferred the signature from the back rather than the correct side. Why it was not seen and corrected is difficult to understand, but it is possible that the method used to effect a satisfactory transfer destroyed the signature and made a repeat out of the question.

This restoration took place when Llandrindod Wells spa was at its most affluent. Trips from town were organized to view the restoration work, in transport provided by Tom Norton's charabanc (the same as provided for Sunday School trips) and the trippers are reported to have made a 'very considerable contribution' to the restoration fund.

The path to the church porch continued past the church and out on to the hill. One of the people from that way was accustomed to take a little more refreshment than he could handle at a pub (now the Poplars) that existed a short way into the village from the church, and would make his somewhat erratic way up the path past the church and on towards home.

One particular night one of the local lads had a grand idea: why not get a white sheet, roll up in it and lie across the path. All went according to plan, the victim came across the lad in the sheet whereupon the lad groaned: 'I've lost my grave, I've lost my grave', to which our reveller replied: 'What's t'e want out 'er at this time o' night anyway', stepped over and continued on his homeward way, singing Nellie Dean.

Turning left out of the churchyard we arrive into the arm of the 'h'. First on the right lies the Poplars, which used to be the Police Station. The Policeman, by the name of Morris, owned and rode a Red Indian motorcycle which was the subject of admiration and envy of all the school. Indeed he was the only motorist in the area except Mr. Bennett who owned an Austin Seven tourer, and Mr. Watson of Drainllwynbir who had a Bullnose Morris. They were later joined by Austin Pugh, a son of A.N. Pugh, 'the Shop', who bought and used a van for deliveries and which he painted and lettered in a very distinctive way. Constable Morris was quite a popular man with the local lads as he was a boxing enthusiast and instructor. The combination made crime practically extinct.

At a later date the Poplars became the Rates Office, where the important Rate Collector, Mr. Hicks, lived. He used to augment his salary by breeding and selling Angora rabbits and their fur.

Having people like a Policeman, a Rate Collector and a Doctor, not to mention a Witch, gave us some sort of superiority.

Opposite the Poplars was the shop—Pugh's the Shop—with three sons and two daughters. This was the heart of the village and full of Good Will, Gossip, and Goodies. Bread, butter, a pound of nails, an axe, a dozen nappies or a feeding bottle, a remedy for scour in calves, a roll of barbed wire, or a gallon of paraffin or a 'Pennorth o' toffees', you name it they either had it or could tell you where to get it. A fount of knowledge and information.

Pugh's the Shop

Just past the shop was a sort of courtyard that gave the impression that it was once a stable-yard. In a corner was a tap to the public water supply, spring water clean and cold even in

109

the heat of Summer, and, last but not least, free. Like the rest of the village it was nothing pretentious but sufficient for the local need. Today this yard is bordered by the Village Hall and a couple of houses, one of which might have been a stable at some time. One other building bordering on this yard is, on some old maps, given as The Hearse House. Was this the place where the hearse was kept when 'Welsh John' and his predecessors served the village and the area? Sadly, we did not ask our parents or grandparents who could have told us. Like all youngsters we were only interested in our own age and now, when we would like to know, it is too late.

A little further up the loop of our 'h' was Great House, the Doctor's residence. Dr. Steele was another Great War survivor whose experiences influenced him all his life. What made him decide to settle in Llanbister is somewhat of a mystery. Be that as it may, he was a great addition to the community, had a memory like a filing cabinet, a short fuse and a soft heart. But, make no mistake about it, he was a good doctor and knew his patients and their families, their strengths and weaknesses. If called out he knew what medicines to take with him and he had his own dispensary, but, and here was a big 'but'.

During the war his eyesight had suffered and he used two pairs of spectacles to see to write out a prescription if he himself did not have the necessary ingredients. The joke at the chemists was that the dispenser needed three pairs and a crystal ball to read it! If need be they would phone him and with a few diplomatic questions get the truth. If for some reason or other his instructions had not been followed, he would fly into a rage and his comments would put a navvy to shame. But then a complete change would occur, he became a perfect gentleman, apologised in the nicest possible way, and continued with his doctoring as if nothing untoward had occurred. Needless to say people avoided any chance of this happening if humanly possible, and made sure that his instructions were followed religiously.

One of his patients, the father of a big family, went to see him about a badly swollen foot. When Dr. Steele asked to see the other foot so as to make a comparison, the patient was somewhat reluctant to show it. On the doctor's insistence, the foot was revealed, whereupon the reason behind the reluctance became clear—only the swollen foot had been washed!

I never heard of him refusing to go to a patient, day or night, height of Summer or the depths of Winter. One story is told of him, and I leave you to judge as to its veracity. There was an old lady living alone, and whenever a rough stormy night occurred she would send for him, but, so the story goes, it happened once too often. As was usual the doctor could find nothing wrong, but had prepared a remedy which he administered. To this day no-one knows what that dose was, but everyone knows that she never sent for him again on a stormy night.

Beyond and still climbing was Ithon View, the home of the carpenter and wheelwright. His workshop had a workbench all the way down one side under the windows which were rather dusty and only cleaned when it was considered to be keeping the light out rather than just to let it in! Stored in the end furthest from the door were huge blocks of tree trunks, kept from touching the floor by being placed on battens of waste wood. These were 'Butt Ash', the lower lengths of ash tree trunks destined to become 'Bowks'—wheel hubs. Not only was the carpenter also the wheelwright, he also acted as the undertaker. His dress was much the same as everybody else's except for his white apron which seemed to be always nice and clean. His shop smelled of turpentine and red oxide paint and wood.

It was usual for a village that had a wheelwright to also have a blacksmith, but at Llanbister the blacksmith's shop was halfway to the next village, and so had the work from both—good for the blacksmith, but not so good for the wheelwright. No village was complete without its tradesmen, its shop and post office, vicar and schoolmaster, district nurse and, if lucky, a doctor, and of course all the others that make up a community. But the carpenter and black-smith were an absolute necessity, for country life would soon have come to a standstill without them. Between them they literally kept the wheels turning on farm and road, for virtually all carriages were made of wood and iron by these two important people.

Next up the hill and nearly at the top was the Post Office, kept by J.J. Price, tall, grey-haired and to me quite a distinguished looking man. He was very much a book lover, and almost the local lawyer, always willing to help with advice and knowledge of country practice and custom. He was often referred to as Councillor J.J.

As well as being the post office it was also a farm, and often the post office was left in charge of Mrs. Price, a lady with quite a head of white hair, which to me always looked like a halo.

The carpenter's shop, Ithon View and the Post Office formed three sides of a square which, for reasons which can only be guessed, was at one time called Potato Square.

Pride of place went to the Methodist Chapel, right on the top, with a magnificent view, both up and down the Ithon Valley where the river wound silver in the evening sun, and over the surrounding hills with just a farm or two showing. Being at the top of the hill, up in the clear air, any Welshman or woman could sing here.

From here the road goes down the pitch or hill of Nant-y-Claf, where a 'prill', or small brook, runs through quite an area of scrubland and timber, very shaded and west-facing. As schoolchildren, we were warned to avoid this woodland on account of adders. Imagine the amusement of the local people when a naturalist discovered adders in Radnorshire, and had the fact published to warn them of the danger! At least adders helped to put the village on the map for a short time!

The 'Back Road' was a track which led across the steep land at the back of the village and connected with the road heading off into the country to the east. On this road was a very small place where a Mrs. Brumidge lived, supposedly an aunt of Mrs. Barnet's, but unlike Mrs. Barnet she had no visible means of support. Coupled with the fact that she always wore 'Widows Weeds'—black skirt to her ankles, black blouse or something similar, black jacket, with a black lacy shawl to waist length and, as a final touch, a black hat and veil, it was small wonder that to us youngsters she was the wicked witch of the story book. If we follow this track to its end we arrive at Penrhos, the home of another postman, and another Price.

Back downhill and along the main road past the Turnpike, there is a road off to the right. Half a mile up this side road is a farm called Lower Caerfaelog. There are indications that the site was some sort of burial ground or religious building before the farm came into existence. Strangely enough there was a field belonging to the Turnpike that was supposed to be another prehistoric burial ground. But proceeding on the road north, on the left is a church, the roof of which is almost on the same level as the road. This church, at Llananno, is quite an old building and contains a exquisitely carved Rood Screen. One theory is that it originated in the monastery at Abbey-cwm-hir and, indeed, might have been stolen from there. But I prefer to say that if it came from there by whatever means, it has at least been preserved for the benefit of all of us.

North again, and on the left a bridge spans the river leading off to other villages, but close at hand is the site of a big house called

Castle Vale, once the home of a local landowner, who is no longer with us and, sadly, neither is the house. Its claim to fame is that it became a hotel called The Copper Bottel in a whodunit written by E.J. Millward, a local author, and featuring ''s funny' Constable Greer.

Next on the left is the Blacksmith's shop or Pentis, serving the wheelwrights from both villages as well as a wide farming area. Under the legendary blacksmith's chestnut tree there was often a hotchpotch of machinery, some repairable and some not so, old iron, new iron, old horse shoes and the inevitable post vice. Also in the heap was one other item of vital importance—an inch thick circular iron disc about four feet in diameter with a central hole about a foot across. This tool was used for banding the wooden wheels that were so important in those days.

The wheel was made or crafted by the carpenter to the correct diameter, which was half an inch greater than the internal diameter of the iron band to go on it. The wheel was then laid on the iron disc with the bowk in the centre hole. While this was being done the wheel band was heated. When red hot to the whole of its circumference, it was carried with the tongs, placed on the wheel and hammered down until it was in contact with the disc and fully 'home'. Cold water was then liberally applied and the shrinking iron closed on the wheel until it creaked, meaning the wheel was ready for use.

Often the shop was a dark and somewhat sooty place, smelling of hot iron and scorching hoof horn as it was burned by the hot shoe to ensure a good fit. Generally a blacksmith's shop comprised two rooms—the outer or Pentis and the inner or Forge with one, two (as in this instance) or, in some cases, three fires or forges each equipped with its own bellows (often pronounced Bellis or jokingly as Billewis), anvil and a general set of tools, tongs, hammers, punches and holes.

If it was necessary to weld two pieces of metal together it had to be done on the forge and anvil. This was where art and experience came in. A good weld was never made on a poor fire, and never ever before the anvil had been warmed up by previous jobs.

A clean fire had to be built up, and caution taken of the 'Dross' that sometimes formed in the base of the fire. The appropriate hammer or hammers were placed in position on the anvil, leaving a suitable area for the metals to be welded. The two pieces were placed in the fire, each according to its size or bulk, each in its own tongs, and the fire blown until a snow white glow, or 'glor' as it was called here, was achieved. Time was given to make sure of a complete 'Heat', otherwise the weld would fail.

As heating progressed the metal gained the same snow white glor. If one did slightly before the other, as it could with different sizes, the most forward was drawn back slightly in the fire. Then both pieces changed to a 'wet look' and time became of the essence.

The blowing stopped, the tongs were gripped, the larger or the most forward piece of metal was taken out first with the hammer hand and put on the anvil. The tongs were dropped and the hammer picked up whilst the second hand brought the other piece of heated metal and placed it on the first. Meanwhile the smith has raised the hammer and, as the second piece of metal touches the first, says 'Nothing to it', spits on the anvil and brings the hammer down onto them. When you land on your feet after the bang, the smith has a little smile to himself and says 'What the blazes happened then?'

The smith also provided a source of local information. Farmer A wants a calf, so Smithy is told 'If you happen to hear of one for sale let me know.' 'B.J.'s pony is lame and won't be in the trotting race next Saturday.' 'Mrs S asked me to tell you ...'

The smith also usually had the best garden in the village on account of the horses leavings in the pentis while being shod!

The blacksmith was a strong man, sturdy and broad shouldered, with a sooty cap, dark shirt and sleeves rolled up above his elbows, his hands dusted with ash, and generally bearing the marks of his trade. With a leather apron fastened around his waist and hung around his neck with a piece of thick cord to avoid his clothes being burned by flying sparks from the hot iron, especially when welding was being done.

A little further up the road, where the valley widens, it is possible, after a climb, to see an old castle mound with a small amount of standing wall. This is the site of Dinboeth Castle. The story goes the the site was considered very important, but there was no water supply. So a pipeline was built to carry water from high up on the other side of the valley. When the castle was besieged, the attackers couldn't believe how those inside were holding out without a water supply. Then, as is often the case, information was gained by trickery or bribe as to the existence of the pipeline, and once the pipe was cut the castle soon surrendered. It was said that

The remains of Dinboeth, with visitors

a line of thistles grew where this pipe went, but there is no sign of this today. If it did exist it may well have been destroyed by modern farming methods.

There were three regular users, other than private cars, of this main road. First there was the 'Mustard Pot', the bus. Yellow as you will have guessed, but guess what else—it carried twenty people at once! It ran twice weekly, on Tuesdays and Saturdays. Never was there a Tuesday that we missed seeing the Mustard Pot go by, providing of course that it had not broken down, which sad to say it did quite frequently. When it did it put our whole week out of joint, not to mention the passengers waiting at the roadside. At some point the owner had to give up the service on account of having tuberculosis, a serious illness at this time. Luckily a local businessman, a shopkeeper and watchmaker, took the route over.

In the goods line there was the 'Vulcan', a lorry that like the bus was a wonder and a sight for sore eyes. It could carry a ton weight and you could hear it coming from at least five minutes away, easily sufficient time for us to reach the road to see this wonder of modern times roaring by at fifteen miles an hour. It had solid rear tyres and pneumatic ones on the front. We thought they were joking when they said the front tyres were full of wind!

The other regular vehicle was the Brooke Bond Tea van. Tall, red and square with BROOKE BOND TEA painted on both sides

115

and, like the others, the driver sat up in his cab like Punch in a Punch and Judy booth. The engine was a Trojan two cylinder which made a distinctive popping sound. The rear wheels were driven by a chain and the back axle was fixed on a solid shaft so that when turning a tight corner one wheel had to skid to compensate for the different distances travelled.

All the vehicles had quite distinctive sounds, so that if we didn't want to be seen by the policeman or the schoolmaster we could promptly do the disappearing trick.

Similarly the approach of a strange vehicle was recognised and all haste was made to see it go by. One rare visitor in this group was the Shell tanker delivering paraffin to the shop. It wasn't a true tanker, just a lorry with a tank fastened on it and on which the word SHELL was painted. Once, to our amusement and delight, when delivering a load one rear wheel crushed a culvert pipe and the lorry became stuck there overnight.

As we return through the village I think of all the memories that it conjures up: posting letters at 1d, postcards at $^1/_2$d; I can almost taste the shop's sweets now, they don't taste the same anymore; a loaf of bread to take home, not quite enough of home-baked to last out, 4lbs weight and cost 9d; shoes to take to Tom Mills'; a dress to collect from Mrs. Barnet. The people we met, talked with, laughed with. Some we pleased, some we didn't, some we liked, others not. What a web of chance and necessity our lives are made of, often without thought, sometimes without reason, all added together to make a lifetime.

Often, when elderly people get talking, you will get two very distinct impressions of their conception of what things were really like in their young days. It nearly always begins with 'I remember ...' and that is where all likeness ends. Memory, like everything else, is subject to the ravages of Father Time, and it is hard to tell whether there are different circumstances in the time remembered or whether the difference is on account of the individual's situation and point of view at the time.

I have heard different accounts of Uncle Jim. 'Uncle Jim', actually not an uncle to me, was a great uncle to my father. He normally lived with his brother, but spent a lot of time away from 'Home', working, even though he was very crippled with the 'Rheumatics' and walked with the assistance of two sticks. One stick was a bit different to the usual, as it had a small spade-like end that went by the name of mole spade. The reason, and as always there was a reason, was that he was the champion (unofficial of course) mole catcher of the district.

Uncle Jim was given the job of building a 'French' barn (with an apex roof) for my father, and for a little relaxation he laid a few mole traps. I accompanied him and soon we became inseparable. Wet or dry, in or out, where he was I was, and even at that age I'm certain that unknowingly I learned quite a lot, except how to catch moles.

The barn's roof was supported on poles twelve feet high and appeared to be a task far and away beyond the capabilities of a person, semi-illiterate and sixty plus, but don't you believe it! All the tools he had available were a hand-saw, crosscut saw, brace and bits, axe, chisels, pocket knife, a ball of strong string, a wine-type bottle (marked up for a level), a lump of 'Raddle', a two-foot rule, a heavy hand hammer and the ability to sharpen and set the saws and sharpen any cutting tool.

Sadly, with the demise of the older methods and tools the associated skills have disappeared as well—the tailor-making of a scythe for it to be an efficient tool, or the hanging of a wooden gate so that it falls shut gently against the 'falling' post, yet stays fully opened when required.

These craftsmen's pleasures were of a quiet nature—a nice animal to take to market that they were proud of, a nicely turned out family taken to Chapel or Church of a Sunday and a hymn well sung at a choir practice on a week night, and most of all the satisfaction of getting a cheque that covered the next half year's rent.

Beyond the village, in the valleys around, were yet others who formed a more distant part of the local community. To the east, Maelynaidd was an ancient cantref in the peninsula of Fferllys. Being open land it was subject to squatter's rights where a young couple could claim all the land that they could dig a ditch around and on which they could erect a sod house and have smoke rising from the chimney by daybreak. The greater the number of friends and relations they could assemble, the greater amount of land that could be claimed—often about 8 acres.

As time went on these crofter's plots were amalgamated and in time became viable farms. An example is a farm called 'Tyler's' which is an amalgamation of a number of plots, including those originally called 'The Wheelbarrow' and 'White Walls'. Others included 'The Temple', 'Wellington', and 'The Ark'—a joking reference to the story of Noah landing on an isolated hill. The Ark, or Llwynpentre as it was sometimes known, was the home of John Richards, or John Jones as he was sometimes known, the mayor of Maelynaidd. He was married but had no children, which was maybe for the best as the marriage became a little vociferous at times. Sound carries an extraordinary distance in certain circumstances and in these resulted in broadcasts of what was supposed to be private, if forceful, conversations. The final and closing statement from John Richards was invariably, 'Thee's marry me for my money, and that thee't never get.' Suffice it to say that she outlived him by several years.

Then there was 'The Boot and Slipper', actually a boot factory making boots for local people and which employed six or seven people. It is now known as 'Pant y Efail' (Hollow of the Blacksmith). Possibly a blacksmith followed the shoemaker, but as is often the case, only a grass covered mound of stone is left to mark the place where people lived and brought up their families.

Curiously the names of these crofter's places were about equally divided between Welsh and English.

While the land was open and unfenced, it was supposed to belong to the Lord of the Manor and hill rent was due annually. On Moelfre Hill was a quarry where the farmers with the right to 'turn out', or grazing rights, attended to pay their Crown Rent. In the quarry was a hole, Craigy Hole, in which they placed their money and from where it was collected by some unknown person.

Near the village lived 'Bill' Weale, short of stature, bandy legged, nasal of speech and roughly clad as he needed to be for his, should we call it, profession. He was self-educated enough to write to prospective customers as to the date and time of his attendance, for Bill was the gelder or, to farming people, 'the Castrator'. This was an essential service to the farmers in the district for gelding bulls, stallions and ram lambs before they reached maturity.

The story is told (of which I do not guarantee the authenticity) that the vicar happened to be going the same way as one of Bill's sons and took the opportunity to instill a little Biblical knowledge where no doubt he believed it was lacking.

'Jimmy', (we'll call him that) 'see those bullocks in the field. Who made them?'

'Alright Parson', says Jimmy, 'I know what you're thinking. 'E made 'em bulls, Dad made 'em Bullocks.'

On his Triennial visits gelding bulls and ram lambs, Bill would recount incidents of note, gossip, genuine news of marriage, pregnancies, quarrels and fights. On account of the large area that he covered and the people he met on his travels over the greater part of four parishes, he furnished a news service that was unique. Some of these incidents would be embroidered with a little 'Weale-ism' here and there just to add a spice to the story, but the 'additions' were harmless and were given and taken in good faith.

There was another angle to this story telling, for they often provided a diversion and cover for a little sleight of hand when a small portion of 'small meat' or a couple or so sweetbreads from the lambs found their way into certain pockets. Everybody knew about it and he knew that they knew, but he didn't charge a lot and the stories were worth it, so no-one cared. When on his way and passing he was always welcome for a meal or a cup of tea.

Unlike Bill, George Goode was a mystery. I always had the idea that he belonged to or was related to well-to-do people, but had got himself lost for reason or reasons unknown. He lived in a corrugated iron shanty up the valley of the Dwrddu, the small brook that joins the Ithon to the west of Llanbister. He was always smartly dressed, in a deerstalker, well-cut jacket and waistcoat and wide thigh-type britches, polished leather leggings and boots, topping off his gamekeeper look with a double-barrelled shotgun under his arm.

I never remember seeing him without the gun, in the village or out on the fields, and as he had no land of his own it gave the idea that he had some dark reason for carrying it. Rumour had it that he was not always as sober as he might have been and during one of those times he was supposed to have threatened someone. Needless to say people were a little wary and left him to his own devices, doing as the old saying advised—'Let Goode Be'.

In the upper reaches of the Bachel brook, about as far as one could get from any farm or village in that district, lived Thomas Bryan. He was not quite so much of a mystery, but still a little different, living in a little tumble-down out of the way cottage, Troed-y-rhiw.

He was noticeably tall, indeed very tall to us as most of the local people tended to be on the short side. He also always seemed to be standing very upright, but this again could be by comparison as farmers and heavy workers tend to lean forward and this was the usual stance. He was always a loner.

Only part of his cottage was watertight and in there he had a bed of bracken and made himself a crude but warm and dry home.

He looked after himself completely and bothered no-one. Whether he had a private income, or if so where it came from no-one knew, and as was the custom of the neighbourhood, nobody asked. What was known was that he had been a reporter for the *Times*, had been unfortunate enough to have suffered a nervous breakdown, and had come to the area to recuperate on account of the total difference to his previous life. Why he stayed is anyone's guess but stay he did as long as he lived.

I suppose he could have been called a drop-out, but he didn't expect anything but what he got for himself. He wasn't a tramp, he wasn't a gypsy, more a recluse, liked and respected, but very much a man on his own.

Archie was a different sort again. He had apparently been a professional footballer for Arsenal, but was now a drover. Whether the same sort of thing happened to him as to Thomas Bryan I shall never know—another mystery!

The difference to Thomas Bryan, though, was that Archie was a worker, and earned his living. A true nomad, sleeping where the day's end found him, be it in barn, byre or haystack—somewhere warm and dry was good enough for Archie, and of course Turk. Turk was his dog, black and white—shining black and white—bright eye'd and intelligent, reliable and loyal, as good at his job as any sheepdog trial winner. Cattle or sheep to Builth, Rhayader, Penybont, Knighton or Newtown, Archie was your man, unless, of course, someone got to Archie first. Then you drove your own.

Then there was Mollie, the original land girl. She dressed in men's clothes and did a man's work, taking any job on a farm where there was a job to be done. Apparently she always had plenty of work.

Like many of us she had her peculiarities. When asked to wash a floor (stone or slate) she always started at the door and washed her way to the fireplace, whilst everyone else washed the opposite way, starting at the cleanest place and ending with the dirtiest by the door. One thing Mollie was very fond of was salt herrings, and if you had a box Mollie was a willing worker.

But I don't know where Mollie lived—as far as I can ascertain she had no permanent place of residence, but just took a chance of finding somewhere to sleep where she found work.

Another casual worker was called David Moses, though his true name was David James. He always arrived in time for the mid-day meal and of course had some dinner, preferably a huge one, before he started. Someone once made a wager with him that he could not eat 4lbs of farm style apple dumpling after his dinner. The wager accepted, David Moses tucked into the first course, which it is presumed was of generous proportions. Then came the dumpling, and anyone who has experienced a good old farm dumpling will know that it is a good solid pudding. Call it a sweet and no-one will know what you are talking about. But it went the same way and David won the wager. However, an hour later he was discovered lying under a hedge, holding his tummy with both hands and begging, 'If thee't hold this once I'll never put on thee so heavy ever again.' He survived, but apple dumpling was a subject best avoided thereafter.

Sarah Lewis, my grandmother, was the local nurse, mid-wife and undertaker's assistant in as much as she 'laid out' the deceased in preparation for placing in the coffin. She had no formal training, only learning by assisting her predecessor.

Dr. Davies, the doctor before Dr. Steele, wished her to take the midwifery exam, but she refused because she then felt she would be obliged or compelled to carry on and do as she was told, whereas she preferred being free to do as she wished.

In the end, 'rules and regulations' meant she had to discontinue what was both her pleasure and largely her life's work, much to the displeasure of local people who continued to seek her help and advice when they thought it necessary.

Dr. Davies had a daughter, Mrs. Ellis, who spent some time in Africa where a son and daughter were born. She returned to Llanbister, built a bungalow and settled down. She used to give us talks in the old school about Africa, which to us was then as far away as the moon seems now. What seemed so strange to us children, was the fact that she had been so far and survived, in fact she was seen as a likely user of the broomstick.

Her bungalow was also something new to us, especially as it had one large room used for entertaining and dancing. As far as local folk were concerned, this was odd, and to us children anyone who wanted such a thing in Llanbister was probably more than odd.

Then there were the 'migrant' workers who arrived at certain times of the year for seasonal work. One of these was Old Beale, who was certain to arrive in the neighbourhood in late May or early June. His speciality was weeding corn, and if anyone could be an expert at weeding corn it was him. He came equipped with his own 'Widuck' or in our language, 'Weed Hook'. This was similar to a

Dutch hoe, but only about an inch wide, which he used to cut the young thistles off below or as near ground level as possible, hoping to kill or maim them. Those not killed were at least significantly damaged so that the corn covered them and so made harvesting (i.e. cutting and tying sheaves by hand) a much more pleasant job. He could be seen working day after day in the same field if the infestation was bad, as if he were hardly moving. He never stopped except to eat and bite off a lump of twist tobacco. With food and a place in the hay to sleep, his needs were catered for. He took his pay when the job was done and went on his way until next year.

As for the farmers, their great ambition was to end their farming days better off than they started and they were willing to work hard to achieve it. The story is told, and incidentally it is true, of a very hard working farmer getting on in years who was heard to say 'I dunna give a cuss as long as I can die worth more than auld Tum the Nant'. The fact that everyone could only guess how much auld Tum left, made no difference. It was an ambition that hurt no-one.

Phrases

These phrases were in general use in the 1920s and 30s but not necessarily confined to the area. Words such as munna, (must not) seem to be due to making some economy of sounds: 'You munna say dunna, it inna perlite; You dinna say tinna cause it binna right.' Generally this sort of language was used by local people when talking to each other and was discarded for almost another language when away from home with a few exceptions, who then were unfortunately then considered backward, or un-educated.

'To Send Visitors'—walking a little way with anyone who has come visiting on the start of their journey back to their homes.

'Up the wooden hill'—upstairs to bed.

'Pride of the morning'—a light shower of rain about nine to ten a.m. on what is likely to be a fine dry day.

'You hold your foot up'—just wait until you hear it all before saying anything.

'Not so bad considering', 'Not so bad for an old 'un', 'Not so bad' —intentional understatements.

'Kick over the traces'—go against parental control, or custom.

'Oot-'ee?'—will you?

'His last cow has calved'—unlikely to have more money left to him.

'I'll be dankered!'—an expression of surprise.

'Corpse Candle'—mythical light that appears over or about a bog or boggy area and is supposed to carry a message of the death of someone close to the person seeing this light. Generally accepted now-a-days as a refraction of moonlight during a fog (natural or induced!).

'A cruddly (mackerel) sky'—never dry for 24 hours.

'Cooch up'—close up together to keep warm as in bed.

'Right p(y)ert' or 'pert'—active and mentally alert.

'His ducks is (or are) all drakes'—someone who seems to have things go wrong on him, or makes the wrong decisions.

'Stands on a lot of ground'—describes a person who overrates his own importance especially if the person is small in stature.

'Let good be'—if something is reasonably good don't risk doing more if there is a danger of spoiling it.

'Be k(y)nd to your neighbour and cruel to his dog'—send his straying animals home, that is where they are wanted and your neighbour will think better of you for doing it.

'Get a bob (shilling) and keep it'—afraid to take risks in business.

'All wind and water'—a braggart.

'Wood from the neck up'—(self descriptive).

'Creep up your sleeve'—refers to a sly person.

'Hit bottom'—to have done something very dishonourable.

'Short on the long'—poor judgement.

'Long in the tooth'—aged, (referring to telling the age of sheep).

'Acting the long eared one'—being stupid or donkey-like.

'Knows which side his bread is buttered'—doesn't protest and put his job at risk.

'Calves kit, or calves cot'—a section of the farm buildings for small calves which was kept draught free.

'Longi-leery'—tall and thin, especially if of a miserable type.

'Ducks disease'—short in the leg.

'Real old scrat'—hard-working and saving; not missing a chance.

'Fit (feet) first'—boxer or fighter carried out.

> 'If the cuckoo light on the blooming may,
>   Keep your cow and sell your hay,
>   Should she light on the bare bough,
>   Keep your hay and sell your cow.'

What this really means is that if the hawthorn is in flower when the cuckoo arrives the spring growth is early and presages good crops, but if not in flower then the season is late and crops likely to be poor.

> 'March will 'sarch'
>   April will flay,
>   May will come and
>   Drive winter away'

If a very bad winter for animals, particularly hill sheep, they often survive the month of March but for some reason April with its warmer weather and grass often sees the end of the weaker ones.

Words

The language or dialect was quite distinctive and this is not intended to be a complete glossary of the local words, only the ones that I remember being used in my childhood years. Quite a few are different to the ones in use today in that district.

The first group are words which include the letter 'y', as used in Welsh to, broadly, sound like a double 'e'. However, this ee sound is in some cases more pronounced than in others. At no time was this 'y' included in the spelling but only in the speech.

The most common of this type were words beginning with a 'c' followed by an 'a'. Prime examples are cabbage, correctly spelled but pronounced Kyabbage, and cart, Kyart.

Others in common use included:

By g(y)ad—by gad.

C(y)ab—cab.

C(y)abin—Cabin.

C(y)ackle—cackle. (geese)

C(y)anna, or C(y)an't—can not.

C(y)at—cat.

C(y)attle—cattle.

C(y)ag—cag. A triangular tear in cloth from getting snagged on a nail or something similar.

C(y)arlock—local name for charlock, an annual weed.

C(y)awping—a dog barking continuously.

C(y)erf—a slab of hay cut from a rick with a hay knife.

D(y)ern, or Jern—eager, maybe overly so.

G(y)abby—some one with a lot to say, usually more than required!

G(y)affer—gaffer, a term used to describe the 'boss'.

G(y)ander—gander.

G(y)ambo—gambo, a two wheeled horsedrawn vehicle.

K(y)ind—this pronounciation refers to the look of things, crops or animals, Kyind or Un-kyind, good or bad. (A caring person is a 'Kind' person (no 'y').

P(y)ert—pert, intelligent, or bright looking.
Sk(y)em—a thin dull film on water or on a mirror.
Sk(y)im—to skim cream from milk.
Sk(y)rt—skirt.
Sk(y)elt—to roam at night.
Sk(y)ewt—in a diagonal direction.

What follows is a list of local dialect in use in the twenties and thirties. Some may still be used in the district or elsewhere:

A-Feard—another way of saying someone was afraid.
Anunt—to place two pieces together correctly, or to aim in the right direction.
Ascal—a lizzard.
Atto—a shortened way of saying 'have to'.
Bait—elevenses, or mid-morning cup of tea and sandwich.
Bellucking—a cow lowing or bellowing.
Bing—feeding alley between two cow-houses where animals are tethered facing the alley for feeding purposes.
Boedging—making a hedge stock proof with hedging wood.
Boggart—a scarecrow made to look like a man.
Boogan—a scarecrow.
Boond—rope of twisted hay or straw. A piece of strong wire was bended to form a 'z' shape with the angles being right angles and one end formed into a hook or huck in the local idiom and a bunch of hay or straw placed in the hook by one person while a second turned the tool,the first kept feeding in more material while the turning continued and the turner moved backwards as the boond lengthened. In this way a rope was formed, the size and strength was controlled by the operators to suit whatever purpose they had in mind, generally to tie down the thatch on a rick. Sometimes when a lot of boond was required the tool had two short lengths of elderberry branch with the pith forced out as handles to avoid any soreness that would result from the friction when using just the bare wire.
Boont—the action of a young animal bumping its head against the udder of its mother to 'persuade' her to give her milk quicker, or more. (In Boogan, Boond and Boont there is a suspicion of the Welsh 'w')

Boosey—the feeding trough for a cow, always at floor level as opposed to the manger for a horse which is always in a raised position.

Brack—a suspicion of or sign of an impending fracture, the first sign of a break in the shell of an egg at the start of hatching.

Braumer (came a)—a very heavy fall.

Brazers—braces to hold up trousers.

Bruck—a local way of saying brook.

Brunt—the worst or the heaviest part.

Bury—a rabbit burrow

Bummer—the Boss.

Caudle—when boiling meat, bacon in particular, occasionally the pot would boil over and the liquor and the fat will spill and run down the outside of the pot. Any water based liquid boils off in steam, but the fat mingles with the soot adhering to the pot and forms a black greasy deposit—the caudle—which was used to blacken and soften leather boots and harness.

Cleese—a collective term describing a cloven hoof or hooves of sheep, cattle etc.

Clooking—a clooking hen was a broody hen, clooking describes the sound she makes as very distinct from a hen 'checkling' when an egg had been laid.

Cooch, to cooch up—to close up together to keep warm.

Copsil—a device on the front of a horse drawn plough to offset the fall or slope of the land, generally in the shape of a quadrant with a pegging arrangement to keep in position.

Crimp—shrivelled and small.

Crink—as crimp, but often referring to small apples.

Crucket—crooked.

Crud—curd, usually when speaking about infection in the udder of an animal when curds occur.

Crowsty—ill tempered, hard to please, bad humoured.

Doubt/Dowt—put the candle/fire out. Another way of saying douse.

Dousting—raining very heavily, At the receiving end of a very heavy snowballing.

Dowl—down, the undercoat of water fowl.

Drawts—a spring balance.

Dunnuck—dung hook, a tool used to pull farmyard manure from a tipping cart some what similar to a fork except that the 'tines' are at right angles to the handle making a hook.

Elder—udder.

Flem—a small stream taken from a river and used to power a waterwheel at a mill or factory.

Flen—any small parasite.

Fitchuck—polecat; a ferret of a dark colour is often referred to as a fitchuck on account of its polecat colour.

Futhering—causing a rustling noise by hunting amongst papers or anything causing a similar noise.

Gawby—a dim-wit or maybe a harmless but stupid person.

Glat—gaps in a hedge where an animal could get through.

Glemmy—warm and damp weather, maybe hot, damp and thundery.

Gobbler—a turkey cock.

Goesunder—jocular name for a chamber pot ('goes under' the bed).

Gonder—another name for a gander.

Goyland, or possibly Gieland—generally refers to very steep land or a clifflike place.

Granchy—crisp and noisy when eating, i.e. as a pig eating raw potatoes.

Hacker—bill-hook, a hand wielded hedging tool.

Hiest—shut up.

Heathering—long slender hedging wood used to weave and strengthen the top of a hedge.

Heulve, haulve, haft or handle—wooden hand hold fitted to the steel component.

Hognal—clumsy or awkward.

Homes or Hames—shaped metal frames with hooks for chains fitted to a horse collar.

Hooling—rooting by a pig.

Hoosin—a leather hood fitted and leaning backward to the top of of the horse collar for the purpose of keeping the shoulders and the padding of the collar dry when raining.

Hoxer or Oxer—when pleaching or laying a hedge, instead of using stakes upright growing wood of sufficient size is cut at hedge height so saving growing timber.

Huck—to hook up, and unhook is 'unuck'.

Ile, (pronounced 'isle')—a shed or small out building attached to the farmhouse and which was generally the housing for the pony and the sheep dogs so as to be available at a moment's notice.

Landtree—a wooden spreading device to keep chains from fouling the legs of the horse when working.

Lap up—to fold clothes, paper etc.

Larpins—children.

Lep—jump, leap.

Linty—listless, a definite dislike of effort, particularly if the effort involved any type of work.

Loun—the width that can be reached by a thatcher to the side of the ladder when thatching a rick or stack.

Lumper—can describe a half-grown animal or children, not small but not yet teen age.

Mawn, Mawn pool—a place where peat has been dug and is now filled with water, often in a boggy place and a place to be avoided.

Mixen—local name for a midden, or pile of farmyard manure.

Moithy—damp and going rotten but not yet soft.

Moither (ing)—delirious, talk that has no sence or reason.

Mosey—similar to moithy but with a mouldy or mouldering smell.

Mulluck—a horrible or untidy mess.

Muntin—abbreviation of mountain pony.

My or Mye—the act of levelling and packing hay or straw in a barn.

Nabel—navel.

Nesh—low resistance to cold.

Nild—needle.

Niscal—the smallest of the bunch.

Noggin—a tinned container capacity about half a gallon (roughly 3 litres), having a handle soldered on one side and used for milking, carrying water to fill the fountain or maybe taking boiling water to 'scald' the butter making utensils.

Ockerd—a mutation of the word awkward but with the meaning intact.

Ool—wool, an instance where the Welsh 'w' double oo sound comes into play.

Oont or Wnt—a mole, again the Welsh 'w'.

Orl—the local name for the alder tree.

Ort—to select the best.

Ortins—what is left.

Perk—roughly seven yards, used as a measure in hedge laying. Seems to be a slight difference with land drainage i.e. tile drains where 3 perk sequals 1 chain, 3 drains at 1 perk spacing, giving a distance of 7 yards and 1 foot.

Petty—soil toilet.

Picrit—pit under the firegrate covered by a cast iron grating, large enough to contain the ashes for the whole day.

Piles—large size stakes used when erecting or repairing wire fences.

Pip—an infection of young chicks about a week old where a worm type parasite gets in the wind pipe and the chick has great difficulty in breathing and unless treated quickly will die of suffocation. A horse hair or a pliable 'bent' was bended into a very small loop and passed down the chicken's windpipe past the parasite and withdrawn, and if you were lucky up came the worm and the ckicken would recover.

Pooning—continuous hammering, or thumping to make a noise.

Prill—a small stream, natural as opposed to a flem which was a man-made stream.

Qualm—a fainting fit or similar loss of sensibility seemingly gone out of fashion!

Queek—(nasty) squeezed hard, but with no lasting harm.

Quiff—a trick or a knack that makes something possible.

Quist—wood pigeon.

Rabbit rack—a path made by the rabbit taking the same route to and from it's feeding ground. Curiously it is composed of separate patches in the grass and are alternately large and small, the small pad by the front and the large by the back paws which pass the front when travelling at speed, front feet using the small pads which ever way the rabbit is travelling.

Roosel—the washing action by fowls and birds in dry dust in an effort to both clean themselves and rid themselves of parasites.

Sally—willow.

Scrat—scratch an itch.

Scawen—elderberry.

Scrawl—another way of saying crawl as a baby does on hands and knees.

Scutch—a coarse and un-wanted type of grass such as couch.

(S)ceech—the sticking together of slack coal when put on a hotly burning fire.

Sheep cratch—a covered wheeled rack with wired sides to give sheep access to hay placed in it and having troughs at sides for feeding of concentrates.

Sheep rack—path made by sheep.

Skit—short and humerous or very much to the point.

Skith—a very light covering of snow on land or ice on water.

Slan—local name for sloe, the fruit of the blackthorn.

Slang—(a) another name for dialect; (b) a long narrow field.

Sledge—toboggan.

Slike—slippery.

Slonch—describes the action of fluid in a barrel splashing about.

Spontle—spots of water or spray caused when falling from a height.

Sprag—to stop the wheel of a moving vehicle and cause it to drag.

Stuckle—four sheaves of oats and six of wheat or barley leaned together to form a sort of pyramid to dry and harvest.

Sprigs—(a) small nails used to fasten leather to the soles of shoes; (b) tips or ends of branches.

Spluther—to eject contents of mouth by sneezing or coughing.

Spurt—(a) young shoots of a plant or vegetable; (b) a very quick start.

Squat—(a) the form of a hare or rabbit; (b) a block of wood used to stop a wheel and the vehicle running backwards down a hill while the horse has a rest.

Squit—talking rubbish.

Stelch—up-right pole to which the cow's tie chain is allowed to slide up and down by means of a ring around it.

Stank—to dam up a stream.

Sucker—a young foal.

Threshal or Thrashal—a flail used for threshing the grain from wheat, barley or oats on the stone floor of a barn, often by two men facing and using their flails alternately with perfect timing.

Thraping—a heavy beating, or as often described as 'a good hiding'.

Thrave—twenty-four sheaves of hand tied wheat.

Tiddling—an orphan lamb reared on the bottle, sometimes referred to as a cade lamb.

Trow (as in cow)—trough.

Tollent—could be called the upstairs over a cow house and filled (myed) with hay for cattle feed.

Trouse—wood for hedging usually hazel, hawthorn or blackthorn.

Tug—a short chain from the 'holmes' to a hook on the shaft of the cart.

Tushing chain—a chain for dragging trouse or trees (a tush).

Yeow—ewe, a somewhat obscure influence of the Welsh 'w' again.

Yorks—strings tied around the legs of the trousers to keep them out of the mud or wet grass, but often said if asked was 'to keep the dust off their knees.'

Vase—('a' pronounced as in 'day') threads coming away from the cut edge of an un-hemmed piece of cloth.

Waggon—a humorous allusion to a chamber pot.

Wangle—not a very straight process or deal.

Whisk—a parasitic infection in the breathing of young cattle making breathing very difficult.

Whitty—another name for the rowan or mountain ash.

Wiblin—small and/or undersized.

Wilgil—of indeterminable sex.

Wisket—a large wooden basket (similar to a garden trug) woven from split wood, oak with a rim a long wild rose briar.

Wythe—a wire around a post and the gate to keep the gate closed but above the top rail so as to be lifted up over the 'head' of the gate to open it and replaced to fasten shut. Possibly the original was wood and so we have the whitty or mountain ash.